The best therapy: A guide for wounded healers

By Jim LaPierre LCSW, CCS

© 2020 Fierce Invalids Publishing, Brewer, Maine.

All rights reserved. No portion of this book may be reproduced in any form without permission from the publisher, except as permitted by U.S. copyright law.

To Brigitte, who makes absolutely everything possible.
To Negley, and Tara, the chosen moms who inspired my belief in self.
To Sheila who encourages and supports like no other
To Zac and Jamie for being my best friends.
To my current best friend, Keith for your love and support.
To my incredible staff/family at Higher Ground
To every client I have had the honor of serving, every colleague I've ever embraced, and my friends in local recovery communities: thank you for all that you have taught me and helped me to become

Introduction

      I was in the middle of a therapy session when I realized I'd lost my wedding ring for the first time. My mind raced suddenly with thoughts not at all related to my client: where could the ring be? How could I have been so fucking careless? I was panicked—but I also had a job to do. We were deep into grieving the love of my client's life. I tried to stay focused on him, what he was saying, what he was feeling.

But the horrible sinking feeling in my gut wouldn't go away—and it was all too familiar. I lived with that feeling constantly. The details of what caused the feeling changed, but the feeling itself stayed the same. In this case, I anticipated the look of disappointment in my wife's eyes. She'd chosen that ring for me, and I'd lost it.

      I rarely experience that sensation anymore. I've done multiple tours in hell. I've been investigated for crimes I didn't commit, fired for things that should have gotten me promoted, survived threats against my license, and been hit up for favors by people who conveniently forgot that they had fucked me over. After all that, I laugh now at what used to paralyze me.

      The second time I lost my ring, I'd learned to marvel at the absurdities of my life. I had walked into the men's room of my agency to find a geyser exploding out of the faucet. A little boy had somehow dismantled the sink. Despite having the mechanical ability of a turnip, I tried to fix it. And in the process somehow lost the ring again.

I gave up a minute later and placed an emergency call to our plumber. By then my shirt was soaked, and I was late for a session. I went into my office, where my client was already waiting. She laughed, so I did too. She didn't mind if I did therapy wet, so I didn't either. Instead of freaking out about the ring, I just texted the plumber to see if maybe he had found it in the drain.

What I've learned is, if you know how to laugh at yourself in healthy ways, you'll never cease to be entertained.

I've been supporting trauma and addiction recovery for twenty years. I entered the field believing I was immune to burnout, vicarious and secondary trauma, and compassion fatigue. I am a slow learner with a high pain tolerance, so it took me years to figure out I'm as susceptible to those pitfalls of the profession as anyone else. I am not Superman. You aren't, either. And we do ourselves, and our clients, a huge disservice when we pretend otherwise.

By the same token, too often in therapy we subscribe to the notion of us and them—"us" being therapists and other professionals, "them" being the clients we're supposed to serve. But there is not, cannot, be any separation between us.

In all my work and writing, I refer to "we" and "us." I don't want any degree of separation between myself and those I serve. Our clients are not "populations" or "those people." They are our brothers and sisters. They are my people. They are people like me. They are folks who look into my eyes and say beautiful things like, "Me too." I am at my best as a therapist when I recognize myself sitting in the chair across from me.

We all want good things to come out of the shit we've endured. I crave ripple effects, and so with what I hope to be genuine and sincere humility, I share my victories and failures with you.

Healthy People Don't Work in Healthcare

Here's why we shouldn't pretend—or worse, convince ourselves—that we're significantly better off than most of the folks we serve: because we aren't. We're all various degrees of unhealthy. That's why we're in this business in the first place. Among those of us in the trenches, it's the worst-kept secret: we're all bananas. With few freakish exceptions, no well-adjusted child ever grew up to be a social worker, nurse, or therapist.

But the rigid hierarchy of healthcare reinforces the fiction of "us" and "them." Credentials and personas dictate everything, and in order to maintain the façade of control and expertise, we act as though we know more than we do, are capable of more than we are, and have our shit together when in fact we're coming apart at the seams. And this is true for everyone, no matter where you exist in the hierarchy. I'm fortunate to be about three-quarters of the way up the ladder, but the folks around me near the top are every bit as burned out as the C.N.A. working triple overtime shifts. We may hide it better, but we're still fucked.

Our hypocrisy is our downfall. We do not live as we advise our clients to. We give away the very things we want to receive, and steadfastly avoid meeting our own needs.

Everyone knows you can't pour from an empty cup, yet we keep trying. My old way of dealing with the empty cup was to rip myself open, bleed into the cup, and then I had something to give. You know the routine: ignore the costs, do more, do it better, serve greatly while you're dying inside. Ten feet tall, bulletproof, with your heart in a thousand pieces.

Our occupations are an application of reductionist philosophy. It feels good to give; it feels selfish to receive. We're all laboring under the desperate (and mistaken) hope that contributing to the healing of others will make us feel whole and happy. Healing is a selfish act—in the best possible sense of the word—and yet we think it can be facilitated by people who are largely selfless. This appears noble. It's not. And while our professions are honorable, our approach to them isn't. It cannot be managed nor sustained.

Let's cut to the chase: We will not optimally teach what we have not learned and more importantly, lived. We all want to be optimally effective. But we ignore an obvious truth: we serve intuitive and instinctual folks. They see the struggles and pain we keep hidden.
They know we're not practicing what we preach, and this undermines everything we try to do for their benefit.

And this is our conundrum. We may be okay with failing ourselves, but we cannot tolerate the idea of failing our clients.

To us, they matter. They have value. We see them in exactly the manner in which we should have been taught to see ourselves. So in order to serve them effectively, we must learn to see—and treat—ourselves with the same respect and love.

You don't have to change for your own sake. You can do it for those you serve. There's no bad reason to start on this road. I came back from burnout multiple times. I changed because I got sick and tired of being sick and tired. I hate being a hypocrite, and ultimately I resolved that it simply was no longer an option to continue as I had. I started taking the advice I gave: better nutrition, sleep, exercise, and most of all, showing greater vulnerability and accepting far more support from those who love me.

I can almost feel you saying, "I'm different. I'm always okay. " I believed that too. I was wrong.

Crazy People Make Babies

My own story starts with a narcissist falling in love with a chronically depressed codependent. They married, had children for what were assuredly misguided reasons, and set about ignoring them. There were three takeaways from my childhood:

1. I don't matter. (so, I set out to prove otherwise)
2. Love must be earned (but cannot be retained)
3. Whatever I did was only worthwhile if it involved copious amounts of suffering.

Fast forward through moving once a year, being bullied throughout elementary, middle school, and early high school. A brief pause to note the substance abuse of adolescence. Arrive at blue collar, working-class poor guy, married with two kids at 22.

I was a delivery driver, (extremely codependent) husband and (completely terrified) father. Fear and codependency meant I could never do enough. Each week, I worked 80 hours and did stuff with my kids 60 hours. I never slept, never did anything to take care of myself. I lived in a constant state of burnout, running perpetually on high-octane terror.

Then, in 1994, my brother bought me a copy of Tom Robbin's *Still Life with Woodpecker*. The book blew my mind.

Shortly thereafter I received a hand me down computer, and became part of an online group of Tom Robbins fans. One of the group members learned of the volunteer work I did at my kids' school and asked why I didn't do that for a living. I made some bitter references to being poor and uneducated. She happened to be a philanthropist (not to mention, the mom I'd always wanted), and just like that, she sent me to college. I went from being a 30-year-old with a high school education to having a graduate degree in four years.

Like most of us, I went out into social work completely petrified, but hopeful that I would receive great support and wise counsel from my colleagues and supervisors. What I experienced (with a handful of important exceptions) was a collection of really fucked up people working in organizations that felt just as fear-based and dysfunctional as my family of origin. I discovered that my colleagues were pretending they weren't obviously mentally ill, addicted, self-destructive, and various shades of neurotic. I worked for five agencies long-term before starting my own.

I was fired by three of them (two of them after I had given my resignation). I had a complaint lodged against my license for "stealing" clients from a former employer (agencies treat people like property). I was threatened with being arrested if I ever returned to a former agency because I "stole" two of my coworkers when I left (why the hell would I want to come visit after being fired?).

I've walked into a lot of unhealthy situations and run into a lot of walls. I've been propositioned for affairs more times than I care to recall. I've been offered drugs regularly and have had to explain countless times why I don't drink. I've covered for coworkers having panic attacks and been threatened by unethical supervisors.

I never wanted my own business. What I wanted was to work with people who were genuine and who could at least be open about their brokenness, if nothing else. And what I learned was that our profession is so broken, if that's what I wanted I would have to create it myself.

Deep down, people like me believe that if you ignore painful things, they will go away. This is true not only of emotional pain but physical maladies as well. In my blue-collar days, I did a lot of damage to my back and knees. I unwittingly lived with a torn artery behind my knee for over 20 years. The pain was never all that bad until seemingly overnight it became unbearable. Eight surgeries later, I had to tell my doc to stop trying to save it for aesthetic value only and cut it off.

I returned to my clients after two months in hospitals. Most of them were at a loss. The tables had turned. They looked at my loss and didn't know how to proceed. To each of them I explained, "My scars show. Yours don't. Both of us deserve to heal."

I move toward acceptance at the pace of a glacier. The lessons appear repeatedly, and the cost of not learning them is always progressively more painful. It has to hurt me sufficiently before I come to acceptance. I had to struggle for years before I realized I needed to work for myself. I had to lose a leg before I knew what I needed to be well.

But we don't always have to learn the hard way: we can find wisdom in the experiences of others, and avoid pains that in truth are optional experiences: strife, agony, dread, intellectualizing, complicating, and avoiding.

Opportunities for reflection and journaling:

- Connect with your intuition. What are the lessons you've been avoiding of late?
- How often do you tend to tie yourself up in knots?
- How's your balance of humility and self-affirmation?

Fuck Depression

I avoid talking about my depression until I feel it surfacing. This is because when I'm well, I'm secretly hoping the depression will never return. Perhaps if I never speak of it, it will never come back. A therapist would call this "magical thinking." It's understandable when kids do it. When adults do it, it's just another way we set ourselves up for failure. I'm never going to walk in the light of day without my shadow.

I spent a brief time in the throes of a depressive episode recently. And that's the best I can hope for—not that it won't return, but that when it does it will be brief. I used to be in it for months at a time. These days it's down to about several hours on average and a few days at worst. Sometimes I can catch it within 30 minutes.

I felt profoundly alone for the first three decades of my life. Loneliness, for me, feels like a 12-year-old boy who has locked himself in his room. He's listening to loud music - to cope and to avoid hearing what's happening down the hall. He doesn't expect anything to ever get better; he just wishes he could have a fresh start and some actual friends.

He's a dorky kid wearing hand me down clothes and thick glasses. He's bright, hyperactive, uncoordinated and socially awkward. He needs a dad but only has a distant father.

He pities his mother but doesn't understand that she could choose differently. He's a great kid but he doesn't know it.

He grew up ashamed, and it endured well into his adult life. It's so common it would be a cliche if it weren't so tragic. Internalizing the rejection of parents and peers leads to perpetual rejection of self. We're ashamed because of other people's failures and cruelties.

As an adolescent and adult, I wanted nothing to do with men. I saw them as untrustworthy, and I believed them to be indifferent toward me at best. The idea that a man could genuinely care about me was a completely foreign experience.

I have always loved women, if in a severely codependent and nonreciprocal manner. I only ever gave, I was not programmed to receive.

It's not hard to see why my loneliness was so profound and why I was perpetually drained, but for the life of me, I couldn't figure it out at the time. I had some pretty huge problems with the guy who's responsible for my happiness. I was too busy avoiding and destroying him to address any of his needs.

Doing good was the only thing that felt good. It was my drug of choice. Martyrdom was the cocktail I ingested all day, every day. I worked far too hard, denied myself everything, and sought to be the dad that my father wasn't. I took everything to extremes because it seemed like the only way to deal with the ever-present fear that I might wake up one day and be him.

I sometimes forget that my choice sets me aside from a lot of my colleagues. I don't allow any contact with my parents. An occasional email is about all I can take. Everything else hurts too much. I tried for over thirty-five years and it just always hurt. You know all those things you do out of obligation? Visits, phone calls, cards? I got to a place where I just couldn't do it anymore, largely because those who watched me cry or implode after each contact helped me accept that I didn't need to keep subjecting myself to emotional abuse. If you feel obligated to your family of origin, you'd do well to consider who taught you that. Then ask yourself, "Who do I want to feel obligated to me?" Right.

It was an important and painful lesson about false hope. I often joke with my clients that I have to give my parents credit for absolute consistency. They weren't intermittently emotionally available. They were never available. My father was my mother's whole world, and my father never overcame the traumas that left him unavailable to his children. Despite their absolute consistency, I managed to hold false hope that they would somehow someday change and meet my needs. That resulted in maintaining unhealthy expectations, which manifested in chronic disappointment—and disappointment, for me, leads to depression.

After I entered therapy as a client, my father had sent me a letter. He'd talked some things out with my sister and had been given some specific examples of how he failed her. His letter invited me to share my experiences, and I took the bait. What I got in return was outrage, and can be summed up in a single rhetorical question: "What do you want from me?" The answer was: Plenty. But I realized then, finally, that he had none of it to give.

That same year, at 8pm on my thirty-seventh Christmas, I realized I had not made the obligatory phone call home and I decided I just couldn't bear even the thought of doing it. So, I didn't.

Still, I've learned there are good men and some of them really like me. That started with Bob and Bobby, who I think of as the Two Roberts. The Universe did me a great favor by bringing them into my life.

Bob stands forever in my memory as this image: A very tall, broad-shouldered, bald man with a fantastic mustache. He's wearing a genuine cowboy hat, and riding a mountain bike with a man purse slung over his shoulder. Bob was the first friend I had as an adult. He was a goof, but he was also just like me – his whole life focused on being the best dad he could be.

We ended up on a local school board together, and Bob offered me at least a hundred invitations – to lunch, to coffee, to any arbitrary means of getting to know each other. I refused them all. Bob persisted, but I pushed him away because he scared the hell out of me.

I couldn't figure out what he wanted from me. In a beautiful moment of vulnerability, he said it plainly and sadly, "I just want to be your friend. Why won't you let me?"

I often find myself having two conversations simultaneously. One is out loud—an actual conversation, with another human being—and one is within myself. When Bob asked why I wouldn't let him be my friend, in my head I screamed, "Because you're a man, and I fucking hate men!" But I'd seen, from his question, that Bob was broken like me. So these words came out of my mouth: "I'm so sorry. Yes, I'd like that. I haven't had a friend in a very long time."

I've learned that the conversations I have internally need to be brought into the open. I was never conscious of seeing all men as being like my father until I said it to my therapist. I never really thought about how my adolescent friends were kids who were lost like me. Our superficial connection was drugs and alcohol. What really united us was being scared and without sufficient guidance and love.

Bob and I were inseparable for a time. Our wives joked about our "dates." Our time together was about food – buying it, cooking it, and feeding absolutely everyone. Bob very powerfully taught me that there were men like me in the world and that they could be trusted because just like me, the last thing they wanna do is make someone hurt like they've hurt.

Then there was Bobby. He lived thousands of miles away, yet became near and dear to me. In the earliest days of the internet, Bobby was a genius with rapier wit. We connected through the Tom Robbins fan website. Our little group became a family and Bobby (despite his protests to this day) was the coolest of all the cool kids. He seemed to have transcended anything I could imagine. He had great wisdom and perfect timing. His perspective showed no signs of socialized limitations. He was incredibly well read and he could say in three paragraphs what I'd need twenty pages to express.

I wanted his approval like I've wanted very few things in life. It's a common thread among us that we all desperately want to be cool. I was young and scared. The Robbins listserve was a collection of brilliant and creatively talented people. I wanted to jump into the fray of ideas exchanged, but every idea I had was half-baked at best. Bobby eventually took an interest in me. He challenged me to defend a point, think more critically, feel more deeply, and express myself far more passionately.

If not for Bobby, I don't know that I'd have ever written anything more than emails. We've only visited in person on three occasions over the course of more than twenty years. Yet, I'm closer to him than to most people I know. We email each other the way I imagine dear old friends used to write letters before the internet. Here's a snapshot of my life. How's yours?

It took me a long time to understand that Bobby was depressed like me. He was just always making us laugh. In retrospect, that should have been a clear sign—the tears of a clown. Bobby is just like me – born to an unhealthy family and taught to understand himself in a way that was never true. Like me, Bobby finds most people to be painfully dull. He looks around and sees frightened sheep looking for someone to follow. He values artistry and critical thinking, great books, and world traveling. For reasons I don't understand but nonetheless am grateful for, he came to value me. Bobby saw potential within me that I honestly had no idea I possessed.

No one really builds up your self-esteem. That's an inside job. Bobby built up my self-efficacy and helped me take pride in doing things well. My self-worth increased as I internalized how much he valued me.

This is what I pass on to my clients – be open to outside input, allow others to have their own truth, and accept the responsibility of not only *hearing* their truth, but also *receiving* it.

Having people who challenge you is the best catalyst for transformation. The Universe knows that I am both a skeptic of myself and emotionally dyslexic. It has provided a long procession of persistent teachers. In retrospect, I see many that I pushed away and others I held at arm's length. Knowledge creates responsibility. We pick better responses as we learn our abilities.

There's just so much more vulnerability in being the student, especially when the subject matter is yourself, or when your role in a relationship is, by custom, that of the teacher. My children have taught me more than anyone else. It was always safe to be completely open with them, and they got to see me at my best – silly, spontaneous, and unabashedly loving.

The teachers I am most grateful to, though, are a handful of women who expressed rock-solid conviction about my worth: these include two of my chosen mothers. Tara and Negs were both members of the same list serve I met Bobby on. To them, I was someone worth claiming. Their love filled a huge hole in my heart. That they would love me when they didn't have to remains a wonder to me.

The adage that behind every successful man there is a good (and exhausted) woman is more true of me than any other man. My wife and I have weathered more storms and achieved more together than I ever dared dream. To say that she is my rock is ludicrous. She is my lifeline, the person who keeps me grounded, and her belief in me is unshakeable.

In the depths of my fear she tells me matter-of-factly, "It's going to be okay." Years ago, during an especially trying time, I demanded, "But what if I fail?!" Her resolve was palpable. "**Have you met you?** Let's say you do fail, then what? With utter predictability, you will get up and try again until you get it right. It's what you do."

I've since come to believe that failure only occurs when you stop trying. People like me are too tenacious and resilient to quit. The real key for me has been to involve people who can both call me out and meaningfully support me. That's no small feat. I intimidate the hell out of most people without any intent or effort. I need people who love fiercely.

If you're a person who hides, you'll have an eerie sense that I see you. If you're intuitive, you'll see that I pick up on the contrast between what you say and do. If you're observant, my animated affect will leave no doubt as to how I feel about what you're saying. I'm just really, real and most people aren't comfortable with it.

It took me a long time to stop watering myself down. I hate pretending because it reminds me of my roots. I'm a transplant now. I never grew where I was planted. I'm comfortable enough with who I am that I am not threatened by your success, conflicting beliefs, or disapproval.

I know me, and I consistently choose to be fair to me. That yields self-respect and dignity. I accept me, which makes your acceptance something I'll enjoy but not require. I have high standards that reflect valuing myself enough not to spend time with people I don't like.

The more I found my tribe, the freer I felt to be myself. The more genuine I became, the more I was free to learn about and invest in me. I found things about myself that I did not like and changed them. I found things I did like, and developed and amplified them. Seeing myself through other's eyes made all of this possible. I knew that the image I had of me was distorted, but knowing what wasn't true wasn't enough to find what was.

You have to get out of your own way to receive input. Otherwise you'll just deflect anything that feels too good. Then you have to explore deep within to integrate the pieces your chosen family gives you. You will find pieces of yourself that you want to discard. You'll find this is impossible to do. You have to heal those parts to become whole.

The paragraph above describes about ninety percent of what therapy is: Learning to let go, take in, and become whole. Had I not done this work, I'd be extremely limited in what I can do for others. This is artistry and spirituality: A client once asked me what she should do with the broken pieces of her heart. I answered, "Make a beautiful mosaic."

Most people aren't seeking transformation, just covering up the pieces they're insecure about or ashamed of. They adorn themselves with status symbols and pursue manufactured ideals of beauty. Most people seek security in wealth. I'm not most people. Don't ever wanna be. I'm more than good enough. I'm good and becoming greater.

Grab that journal:
- How do you experience mainstream people?
- Are you a misfit like me?
- How skilled are you at pretending?

A History of Mental Illness

My brain does an awful lot of stuff without my permission. It goes 100 mph all day, every day. It is capable of both amazing and terrible things. I had to make friends with it because fighting it never brought a positive result, and medicating it made everything feel empty.

Most of the incredibly interesting and creative people I know have brains like mine. It's lazy to lump us all together under a half-assed diagnosis, but that's what the DSM does with folks like me. And as a healer, I reject such careless shorthand. It makes a lot more sense to me to focus on personal strengths and solutions than on how the problem itself is conceptualized.

The biggest part of making my brain manageable was learning to give it goals to work on and ideas to consider. For twenty years, I have never been without projects of all sizes. I cannot afford to be without them. In the absence of purposeful and passionate actions to manifest, my brain will wander into dark places, go down blind alleys, and take pretty much every opportunity to get itself—and me—into trouble.

My son has the same wiring I do. We were in a sports bar once when a friend asked us to describe what it's like to have brains like ours. Without hesitation, my son gave her the highlights of all six ballgames playing on the 12 tv screens. He described how incongruent the background music playlist contained three different genres, the dissatisfaction of a party three tables away from us, and the behavior of two young children on the other side of the dining room.

When he paused for breath, I nodded agreement and offered that the bartender and manager are having an affair, that our waitress is bulimic and likely an alcoholic and that the couple in the booth across from us are on a first date and it's never going to work out. Now, add to this sensory overload a high level of emotional sensitivity and empathy, and you have an idea of what my brain is like.

And it's like that 24/7/365.

I have to do some mindless stuff in the evening to get it prepared for sleep. Otherwise, my brain will behave like a supercharged rubber ball in a tightly confined space. This is something most of us have in common – bed time is the hardest time for us.

There are no distractions, and we're left alone with ourselves. Our brains review the day, focus on the faults, and connect to past mistakes. Inevitably, this leads to snowballing and culminates in a highlight reel of our worst memories of the past and anticipated fears for both the immediate and long-term futures.

An awful lot of us will wait for pure exhaustion before lying down to sleep. We are sleep deprived and therefore emotionally raw, yet we wonder why everything hits us so hard? We are busy people who externalize time and energy to ensure there's nothing left to look within.

I am brilliant at externalizing. At the time of this writing, I own and operate an outpatient clinic. I am its executive director, clinical director, and a working therapist. I am an adjunct instructor at a local university. I sit on two boards of directors for local nonprofits (Chairperson of one, vice-chair of the other) and actively volunteer in them. I am creating an online treatment program, do ghostwriting for my local newspaper, play poker three nights a week and publish blogs while writing this book.

That's my baseline. (It used to be much worse; believe it or not, I'm getting better.)

Spinning plates -- That's the image I have in my mind when I picture how much I have going on in my life. Every so often, I convince myself that I can add one more plate. Inevitably, there comes a time (every 2-3 months currently) when I take stock of the plates, and I resent nearly all of them. If I ignore this awareness, I am doomed. I will guard only the most precious of plates and tell myself that I don't care if the others fall. But that's a lie I tell myself. I don't drop plates.

It's fucking nuts by any standard. The good news is I effortlessly rationalize doing all this. The bad news is that as I get older, it's harder to sleep. I wake up once or twice a night to pee. At 4 this morning, my brain kicked in and said, "Hey, let's review everything you'll be doing in the next week or so!" My body groaned and pleaded for sleep. I'll be dragging a bit today, and that means extra coffee, which means peeing more, which means less sleep tonight. Patterns are easy to fall into. Mine are conscious choices based in a harm reduction model.

The links between ADD and depression are as underexplored as they are obvious. As my son puts it, "It's hard to find people who are on my level." That statement sounds arrogant, which is one more reason why people like me so often succumb to loneliness and isolation.

It's tough to just say to someone, "I'm looking to connect with people who are smart and very aware, empathic and highly sensitive. I want desperately to relate to people like myself because I need to be understood." Seeking out such folks has never worked for me. I have to trust the Universe to provide them.

Self-examination time:
- What are the quirky ways in which your brain works?
- What are the places your mind wanders to?
- Is it possible you need to develop better places for it to go to?

Empowering Others & Limiting Ourselves

By profession, I am a "social worker." I've never viewed that title as part of my identity. I view any person who is trying to make the world a better place as a social worker. My experience is that most healers and helpers are not nearly as self-accepting as we are accepting of those we serve. We do not attend to ourselves as well as we do to others. We uphold the worth of oppressed people and too often devalue ourselves and our efforts.

In many families, there are two sets of things: one for us and the other for company. There are dishes, crystal, and silver we only use when company comes. We save our best stuff for others. We in the healing and helping professions have two sets of everything:

Two sets of values, perspectives, ways of judging and relating. We have one for ourselves and one for the rest of the world. It's the most limiting distinction possible. We who have great empathy for others, often lack compassion for ourselves. We who seek to change the world are often giving away what we most need to receive. We who seek social justice are often far less than fair with ourselves.

Advocacy and macro-level social work are places we like to hide. Being angry on behalf of others is righteous and intoxicating. One of the most effective social organizers I have ever known would rally the troops, promote legislative action, and celebrate by retreating to his en-suite and adding new scars to his body.

In the midst of all that we seek to change, we must achieve greater awareness of our unmet needs and have a greater willingness to meet them. We must notice how we oppress ourselves and seek both lovingly and pragmatically to do the same for ourselves that which we do for others.

It is not selfish to take care of yourself while serving the world. Quite the opposite: it is absolutely and undeniably necessary. The sooner we stop pretending otherwise the better off we are and, more importantly for this discussion, the better the quality of our work. We all heard the flight attendant say to put your own oxygen mask on first, but we don't do it. **We don't protect what we don't value.**

Put another way: if what we *truly* want is to serve others as effectively and compassionately as possible—if, in other words, the selflessness we lay claim to and flaunt is genuine—then the only path is to care for ourselves first.

Instead, we use humor to cover up our lack of self-care. We make frequent references to the surrealism and irony of our work. We get by—barely—with gallows humor and false clinical detachment.

Years ago, I was in a staff meeting of especially burned-out social workers. We all knew that one of our colleagues was showing serious signs of untreated mental illness, but he was a supervisor, so no one dared point it out to him. He responded to a question about the technology budget by screaming, "I think we need to be a lot more concerned about the drones outside that window monitoring us than getting new laptops!"

The meeting continued as though that were a completely reasonable thing to say. I scribbled a note to a friend that said, "Is it just me or does this feel like having family dinner as a kid?" Whenever we pretend, we're not coping. We're not validating each other's experiences or maintaining our sanity.

In our professions, what we don't know will hurt us. While it's unlikely that we will end up harming a client by virtue of these, they will limit the scope of what we're able to treat effectively.

Even knowing that each of us has blind spots, we don't generally allow others close enough to see what they are and challenge us on them. We're watching out for everyone—but no one's watching out for us. Imagine a car with no mirrors, and then imagine you drive it without ever looking to the side or over your shoulder. This is what we do, every day. This is the practice that has become normalized and codified in our profession.

My blind spots are usually unfinished business: inner conflicts and baggage that I am not yet free of. For many years, I found I could not effectively serve men who were loud and angry if they were older than me. I never saw that this was a trigger. I felt a sense of urgency to de-escalate the client instead of delving deeper and confronting the pain that lies beneath anger. The obvious connections to my father were not apparent to me because I wasn't seeking to identify and understand my limitations. Rather, I was trying to constantly push them away, out of a subconscious reluctance to understand what they were.

My focus was squarely upon the client before me and not at all on myself. I asked all the wrong questions ("What's stopping them?" "Why aren't they receiving what I'm offering?") because they were about 35 to 45 different people instead of the one guy I'm with 24/7/365. I could have been seeking my obstacles and limitations. Instead, I was constantly adjusting to the person in front of me even when I was crawling out of my skin.

It's so simple: Get comfortable with yourself, learn to trust your instincts, let good people support you. If you do those things, understanding and effectively treating others is still hard work, but comes pretty easily. To do this is rare and exceptional—and it is also the only way for us to practice our profession optimally.

Time for some writing:

1. Give me ten strengths and five weaknesses that you embody. Write those out before you read any further (honor system).
2. Of the strengths you listed, how many are stand alone qualities and how many of them are descriptions of who and how you are to others? Let's try it again – ten strengths of who you are. Just you.
3. Those weaknesses you listed? How many of them would your friends agree with? Are they fair assessments of you? Ok, now write out honestly – what are you going to do about those?
4. The connection between self-care and effectiveness is clear. Given this, the best way to ensure you'll be effective in serving others is by improving your self-care. Write out one thing you'll add to your self-care and stick that shit on your fridge immediately.

Be Real or Get Out

In my work with healers, I urge two things above all else: Be genuine and practice what you preach. The world has way too many well-meaning professionals who are largely ineffective. Those who provide the best service are those of us who not only felt broken but who also have experienced a lot of healing. I'm a good therapist primarily because I've received a lot of good therapy. I'm a good teacher because I've had good teachers. In a complex profession, these are simple lessons I make use of every day.

I seek out people who are fucked up like me and work to promote their healing. It's obvious that I do this with clients. But perhaps more importantly, I do it with other healers. It brings me joy that nothing else provides, and it also enables me to exponentially increase the sum total of healing in the world. I can only be in one place, with one client, at a time. A dozen other therapists who think and practice better means there's a whole lot more healing going on than I could ever provide alone.

I spent some time this morning encouraging one of the healers I most respect to examine her expectations of self. We've discovered a theme in which the worse a client's prognosis, the greater her efforts. She sees this as rising to the challenge and craves the most difficult of cases.

The work she most enjoys is exhausting. She serves those who have a very high willingness to work hard and transform, but those folks sometimes plateau or regress. She was feeling guilty and conflicted, having found herself resenting some of her clients.

Her expectations of self were subconsciously developed and therefore entrenched and problematic. Whenever a client stopped making progress for any reason, she pushed herself harder. Rather than considering that perhaps they'd gone as far as they were ready to or that some new obstacle might be holding them back, she endlessly wracked her brain to find ways to inspire further growth. When it worked, she felt accomplished and yet would give all credit to her clients. When it failed, she found herself annoyed with herself and frustrated with her clients for not making further gains.

Sometimes we need a not so gentle reminder that it's not about us. People stall out, develop new goals, and face new challenges. We need to check in with our clients and see how they're feeling about their progress and whether they feel ready to continue. Pushing ourselves endlessly is unsustainable, unmanageable and a recipe for burn out.

I see myself in her experience. What I most crave is a rare combination – a terrible prognosis and high willingness to do the work. I've been blessed to serve people who are not only incredibly resilient but also courageous. They inspire me. They've survived nightmarish traumas but get up every morning and parent lovingly. My people claw their way out of hell like Andy in Shawshank Redemption, which is a perfect analogy for recovery: crawling on our hands and knees through a long dark tunnel full of shit to become free.

My favorite question to ask an intern is, "What do you think it says about me that I'm only drawn to working with the worst prognoses?" Is it my ego that wants to succeed where all others have failed? Is it a form of identifying in which I see those folks as being like myself? Could it be as simple and gratifying as the idea that I'm bored with normal people and I find garden variety therapy predictable and therefore dull? Perhaps it's as my friend Keith frames it, "We are not drawn to the darkness. We love guiding others toward the light."

In truth, I think it's a combination of all of these. I spoke briefly years ago with a local psychiatrist who had a client she was considering referring. She asked about my work and what kind of clients she could send. I was both in a hurry and more than a little arrogant. I explained she should only refer cases in which no past professional efforts had shown benefit.

She did exactly what I asked, which meant on average I got one or two referrals from her per year. I loved every one of them. In retrospect, I see clear commonalities amongst them.

They were all especially intelligent (often a liability in healing and transformation) and remarkably talented creatively.

Getting back to the healer I was serving this morning - she saw reflecting on her expectations of self as an opportunity. I realized for the umpteenth time that it's something I need to revisit again and again. It's not a destination I arrive and remain at. With each new challenge and role I take on, my expectations must be consciously developed and chosen. When I run on automatic pilot, I stop thinking about what I repeatedly do because it becomes what is normal for me.

My normal is excessive. I am far more focused on opportunities than manageability. I spent the first thirty years of my life running away from me – from depression, past trauma, and the ever-present feeling of not being enough. For the past twenty years, I run toward what I love – people like me. That, in and of itself, is not the problem—they're the people I work best with and most want to be around. The problem is that I'm insatiable.

There's a part of me that's always pushing the envelope and always wanting to do and be more. I know and feel that I am enough just as I am, yet I crave further growth and greater ripple effects from my contributions (and by "ripple effects" I mean tsunamis). My passions are many. My desire to connect with those who facilitate healing and those who require it is unending.

Balance is restored when I accept my limitations. As my friends in 12-step fellowships remind me, "You don't have to like something to accept it." My desire to do more and cooler shit is in part, an ongoing attempt to feel more and more fully alive. Today, balance is achieved by asking myself, "This thing that I'm considering taking on, will I resent it later because it's too much?" We're back to the spinning plates. I have to consider how many are already in the air, and how they'll be affected by the one I want to add.

We need to be clear with folks about what they can expect from us and what we expect from them. I have found that I must also have conversations with myself, acknowledging my motives, and what I can realistically hope to achieve. I've learned that that conversation isn't always honest. I have to bring it out into the open to ensure I'm not allowing my heart to choose (as opposed to my gut) and share it with others to ensure accountability.

What do I expect from others? Truthfully, far less. What would I expect of a friend or a colleague? About the same, but with the caveat of wanting them to have tremendous support and self-care. I get to more fully practice what I preach. Do less, be more and get as good at receiving as I am at giving.

Maybe you're like me. Maybe you expect something like this: To be the best person I can be while striving to endlessly learn, grow, heal, and become. To be the best partner, parent, therapist, friend, community member, leader, employer, writer, worker, and poker player I am capable of being. To give generously, lift up those who have fallen or been downtrodden and support worthy causes. To be creative and expressive, genuine and honest. I expect myself to do the right thing at all times and in all places. I expect that I will do what my Higher Power directs me to do and I know that my HP has many purposes for me – not only in the grand scheme of things, but also in my daily life.

Some thoughts to reflect on:

- There is far less vulnerability in giving than in receiving. Who's filling your cup these days?
- Do we expect to fail occasionally? Is it acceptable to do so? Beneficial?
- I often suggest to folks that they write up everything they're currently doing and then imagine it's a job description being passed off to someone who is going to take your place for a time. How does it look in that context?
- Do you ever find yourself resentful of those you serve? How do you resolve this? Is it possible that

you don't? Maybe you only take a little time away and go back refreshed but bitter?
- If someone who loves you knew everything you were doing and expecting of you, what would their response be? (Write it out!)

Who the Hell are You?

I am a wounded healer. That is much more than a role or profession I fulfill. It is a defining aspect of my identity. Facilitating healing is not simply performing a series of actions. It is a calling that reflects my beliefs and values. It is a natural extension of who I am. I have chosen my identity, yet it is constantly being fine-tuned. As a work in progress, I intend to continue learning, healing, growing, and becoming as long as I live.

Stagnation and complacency are constant threats. They lead me away from self-care and gratitude and toward a life in which I am simply going through the motions. Without sufficient mindfulness, habits, and accountability, I will often fail to be less than what I expect of myself. Without sufficient support and encouragement, I will become paralyzed by my fears and pain, and increase my risk of vicarious and secondary trauma. Knowing myself then is not only imperative to promote my success, but also to ensure I am maintaining good health and quality of life.

When I serve healers as clients, I often feel as though they are gossiping. I check in with them. They talk about their lives and their work, but they are speaking of the actions and experiences of a person that in truth they do not know. In the absence of a strong sense of identity, their sense of their work and indeed, of their lives, is completely external. They can accurately identify what is going on in the hearts and minds of everyone they know, but not themselves. Their dissonance tends to be pronounced and leaves both their stress and negative emotional experiences unchanneled.

The healers I supervise know that in each meeting, before we speak of any case reviews, we're going to establish how they are doing and what if any unmet needs exist. This is essential to the success of our practice, which is why we do it first, every time. The professional who is supported and who has strong self-care is likely to do excellent work. **The healer who is not aware of self is going to miss red flags that can only be spotted intuitively.** That's true both about their client's well-being and their own. Do you notice when these warning signs crop up in your own life?

- Subtle: Growing caffeine intake, melancholia, decreased socialization and exercise, minor sleep problems, cringing at a client's name in your schedule, feeling overwhelmed, behind on paperwork by a week or more. Noticing a peer relationship with a colleague feels a lot like a therapy session.
- Moderate: Any use of intoxicants (alcohol, cannabis) to cope with work, resentments against

management, personal time accruing significantly, difficulty leaving work at work, struggles to concentrate, nightmares, ongoing G.I. disturbance and recurring headaches.

- Severe: Realizing you haven't truly absorbed anything your client has said in the past five minutes. Exhaustion. High levels of anxiety. Struggling significantly with transference and counter-transference. Bullshitting your clinical supervisor about being "fine."

Why Do You Want to Help People?

There's a brief but insane conversation that happens over and over in interviews for front-line social work positions:

"Why do you want to go into (the healing and helping professions)?"

Answer: "Because I want to help people."

That's where the conversation ends. As though all the ramifications and implications of that answer are self-evident and healthy (they never are). There's a critical and illuminating follow-up question that unfortunately never gets asked:

"Why do you want to help people?"

That one has stumped a lot of interns and students.

I guest lectured a graduate class recently in which I asked, "Why are you all here?" An uncomfortable silence followed.

I continued, "One of my favorite local AA groups is named, 'We're all here because we're not all here.' Is that true of you?" The nervous energy in the room was palpable.

The instructor was visibly reconsidering having invited me when an especially perky perfectionist offered, "I just find people really interesting." I asked if it was possible that, rather than being interested in other people, she was really studying psychology as a means to attaining a better understanding of herself? She was predictably shaken, and remained quiet for the rest of the class.

I suggested that working in social services is far from an altruistic endeavor. I explained that the more I serve people like me, the better I feel. My fulfillment and honor are in serving. My responsibilities are both serving myself and allowing myself to be served. To ensure that we do no harm requires an understanding of our motives. And our motives are usually only clear in retrospect. I wanted to give what was denied me. I wanted to help kids because I was a kid nobody helped. My motivation was selfish, and self-directed—I never wanted anyone to feel what I felt, nor see themselves as I saw me.

Serving and healing can never be as simple—or selfless—as "wanting to help people." That's too easy, and mostly untrue. If we want to know our real reasons for going into this profession—and thereby be as good at it as we can—we need to do a shitload of work on *ourselves*. In my case, it took years of therapy to become the person I needed when I was a kid, and I remember well the moment when it all clicked. My therapist played a dirty trick on me. She asked me to describe my son, who was nine years old at the time.

I spoke endlessly about how good he was, how perfect and loveable, and about how proud I was to be his dad. I went on and on, while she patiently listened. When I couldn't think of one more superlative to describe him (and it took a while), my therapist shifted gears and asked, "Now, isn't that how you've always wanted someone to feel about you?"

I cried for the rest of that session.

In the next session, my therapist upped the ante even further: she suggested that I was free to treat myself as I did my children. This was some mind-blowing shit. I told her that was crazy.

"Why?" she asked.

"Because they matter!" I yelled, as though the fact that I *didn't* matter should have been obvious.

She smiled sadly and finished the sentence for me: "...and you don't."

I cried for the rest of that session too.

I lived far too long as though my worth had to be proven and love had to be earned. Intellectually, I knew better. I've come to see that in a very real sense, it doesn't matter what I know. It matters what I believe. Today, my choices are rarely based on emotion or insecurity. They are based on what I believe and value.

Everything about changing our lives is easy to understand and hard to do. Every change requires moving out of our comfort zone and away from what's familiar. This underscores the need for kindred spirits. People like me have great intuition, and no matter how fucked up we are in how we see ourselves, we readily see the truth about others.

Ok, grab that pencil and riddle me this:

1. As best you recall, why did you start off on this journey?
2. What do you know now that you didn't then?
3. Why do you continue on this path?
4. Who is in your life that can teach you about you?
5. What do you need to know?
6. Go call them right now and ask.

We're Misfits

The easiest way to explain people like me is through the old animated Christmas special, Rudolph the Red-Nosed Reindeer. Remember the Island of Misfit Toys? They thought they were broken and that nobody wanted them, but they came together and formed a family.

That's those of us in the healing and helping professions. That's how we are. We are different but in amazing ways. Nobody loves like we love. Nobody laughs like we laugh. Nobody will ever be as honest with you as we will. Our loyalty to each other is fierce, and we are the very best people to call at 3 am when the wheels have come off the bus because nobody can be there for you like we can. Despite being so good to each other, we struggle to be good to ourselves.

The world feels very cold when you don't know other misfits. It's not like we're out in the world with identifying tee shirts. We must be willing to take risks in order to find each other. To seek us out requires going to places where people who have truly suffered gather. You must also notice that we are overcoming suffering, moving away from survival and progressively toward living a life second to none.

We can be found in psych beds, homeless shelters, and sometimes in jails and prisons. Some of us gather in AA, NA, CODA, Al-Anon or Nar Anon meetings, and group therapy. You can also find us serving our communities and in places everywhere where people are doing things passionately, creatively, and with great love. It takes a lot of courage to talk to us beyond pleasantries. You must trust your intuition and take a chance.

Some of us can pass for "normal" and some of us just can't. Most healers and helpers transcend "passing." We're placed on pedestals by those we serve. It's hard to admit you're a misfit when you feel like you have to live up to that hype. We get stuck in feeling like hypocrites.

Good news! We're the best kind of hypocrites. We only limit ourselves with our shit. That means the only people we have to get right with are ourselves.

Just keep at the forefront of your thoughts Einstein's words, "Problems cannot be solved with the same mindset that created them." Nor can they be solved alone. We need outside perspectives, accountability, and support.

1. Can you pass for normal?
2. Have you ever examined that? What would it be like if you couldn't?
3. Have you viewed normalcy as inherently desirable?
4. Wanna reconsider that shit?
5. I recently forfeited my ability to pass by tattooing both my hands. What's your immediate reaction to

that? Does it make me brave, crazy, or something else entirely?

Fortunately, I Had Pneumonia

Once, I was so sick that I literally could not do anything. It was the first time in my life that it simply didn't matter how badly I wanted something to happen. Whatever it was, and no matter how hard I might try to will it to happen, my body had one answer: "Fuck you, not doing it." Terrible, right? It was. But it was also a gift of sorts, because I was forced to ask for help and to allow myself to be served. I had no choice, because I wasn't physically capable of doing for myself.

For a lot of years, I served recklessly. I lost sleep, serenity, multiple jobs, countless opportunities, and half of my right leg by disrespecting my holistic health. It never occurred to me that I could run out of such basic things as compassion, empathy, or energy. I hit wall after wall, pushed through each time. Again, I'm a slow learner, and I insisted on learning all my lessons in the most painful way possible. And then I got so sick that I couldn't do a damn thing.

That experience planted a seed. What I know today is that I am old long before my time and I have an abundance of scars that could have been avoided. This motivates me to teach others, in the hope that they will learn from my mistakes instead of making their own.

We all want good things to come out of our pain.

Clinical supervision is how I do most of my transformation. There is no good metaphor for what supervising others is like in this capacity. The closest I can come is that it's like parenting adolescents. You try to protect people who are pretending that they're not scared and that they know what they're doing. You get to be a small part of their development and nothing can make you prouder than seeing their growth and mastery.

The idea is to teach effectiveness, which requires awareness of and respect for self. I want to ensure that my colleagues don't burn out or succumb to compassion fatigue, so the first thing I say to a new clinician is, "You're supposed to be scared shitless. Don't pretend otherwise. For that matter, don't pretend anything. Be real or get out."

That's tough but fair. The hard thing is trying to be yourself when you're not sure who that is.

"I don't care what it costs me." Those words were spoken to me by someone I clinically supervised. It's a sentiment I used to embody. Again, we don't protect what we don't value. If we don't value ourselves, it makes sense that we'll do anything *to* ourselves, at any cost. I certainly did.

There's a fine line between what is clinical supervision and what is therapy. I've been known to play hopscotch with that line. What I knew through observation of this particular supervisee was that she lived with a lot of anxiety and was a consummate people pleaser. What I knew intuitively was that she was a survivor of trauma and that she had no small amount of completely unwarranted self-loathing.

My challenge to her was a positive and truthful manipulation. I told her that she might not place a high value on herself and specifically her self-care, but that her effectiveness as a clinician largely depended upon it. I knew she wouldn't do it for her own sake, but confronting her hypocrisy, vicarious and secondary traumatization, and burn out as detrimental *to her clients* shook her.

I knew this strategy would work with her, because she and I are the same. Give me a reason not to do what's in my best interest, and I'll grab it every time. Show me the path that will help me, and I'll refuse it—because fuck you, and fuck me.

One of the first things I had to accept in serving misfits (survivors, addicts, alcoholics, otherwise self-destructive individuals) is that they can read me like a book. The difference between most healers and me is:

- I know what they're reading
- What they see is that I attained closure and healing but still have scars
- I like me (a lot, actually).

As healers and helpers, we will never be pain-free, and we must never stop growing. Of course, we'd like to just grow on our good days, when it's easy, but that's not how it works. We grow the most when we experience pain. To a lesser extent, **we grow because we learn from bearing witness to the suffering of others.**

Occasionally I still hear myself offering guidance that I don't take. This used to be something I'd be ashamed of or embarrassed by. Now I recognize it for what it is - an opportunity. In those moments I jot myself a quick note to come back to the advice, take stock, and explore what prevents me from more fully practicing what I preach.

We have to write it out and talk it out. In AA, this is expressed as "telling on ourselves." If we don't share the inner conflict; we can't trust that we'll resolve it. In nearly every circumstance, vulnerability with trusted others simplifies our lives and increases the efficiency of change dramatically.

Introspection:
- What are the limits you push most?
- Who are the people in your personal life that you give to but don't allow reciprocity from?
- What's the advice you give but don't take?

The Proctologist Located My Head

My first full-fledged professional position was one I was grossly undertrained and utterly unqualified for. As is often the case in rural service delivery, I was the best of only a handful of applicants. I had interned with the agency that hired me. In retrospect, my willingness to drive to far-flung places and attempt to do good work, more than any actual qualifications, was undoubtedly what got me the job.

I worked in treatment level foster care. I knew nothing of attachment disorders or how to effectively treat children who had experienced sexual abuse. My employer didn't have to throw me into the deep end; I jumped in with both feet and quickly found myself drowning.

Something to consider when you're treading water: whatever you're clinging to should be something that supports and sustains you, not something that weighs you down. As obvious as that is, you'll notice a lot of your colleagues can't accept the life lines thrown to them because they're holding fast to something that makes all of it worse.

In grad school, I had completed a clinical track as a generalist social worker. I left there with the belief that it was reasonable of my employers to expect that I should be able to help just about anyone with just about anything. This is of course, ridiculous. **Each of us, regardless of our education and**

training have aptitude and relative strengths and weaknesses, and the specific work we do should reflect that.

I learned that I could not leave work at work when I served children. My clients were roughly the same age as my kids. I sat with little girls like "Liza" who was sexually abused by members of her "church" from infancy to age five. Liza was a lot like my own daughter. They liked the same dolls, same tv shows, even the same snacks.

Liza and I tried to do play therapy together. Liza would pick a doll or a stuffed animal. She'd love and nurture it as a mother would. She would eventually shift and say things in a sickeningly sweet voice, "Poor, sweet, baby. I love you so much" and then she would scream and beat the doll mercilessly. How do you respond to a five-year old whose play makes you want to vomit? I appealed to her to be gentle.
She looked at me in a manner that inexplicably conveyed an unspoken message with complete clarity: that I didn't understand how life works and how people are.

I would go home and imagine my children suffering as those I served had. It fucked me up. I was compassion fatigued in no time and feeling ashamed that I didn't have more to give.

Since then, I've learned that there are plenty of things I'm good at and a much larger number of things that I suck at. That's okay. I love kids, but I lack the stomach and patience to do therapy with them. I came to accept that I wasn't good at play therapy and more importantly, I simply didn't want to do that work.

Trauma, addictions, and crisis work with adolescent and adults are things I excel at, which is all the more delightful considering that I never intended to do any of these professionally. I set out to work with kids, but moving on to an outpatient setting, I saw diverse populations with a plethora of different conditions.

Here too, I found a lot of things I suck at, most notably, treating personality disorders. Successful treatment requires that a clinician maintain a lot of emotional neutrality and composure. I am a highly animated person on my down days. Put me with someone who lives in self-pity, and they become my mother: sad, completely passive, and resigned to a melancholy life. I become a rageful cheerleader who refuses the powerlessness of changing others and devote a lot of time and energy into convincing them that they can have so much more *if they'd only try*.

"Penelope" was a good example of this. She was nineteen, an open-and-shut case of Histrionic Personality Disorder. Only two things ever earned attention from her dad and other father figures: being sick, and being available for sex. Her narratives were consistent: everything was hopeless. Her behavior was consistent: "I'm cute. Why don't you want me?" My responses were consistent: "We're never going to have sex. How about being resilient and trying some new things?"

Penelope received relatively worthless treatment from me because I was not willing to accept my limitations—specifically, that I was not well-suited to serving clients like her. I was well-meaning but misguided, trying to dispense hope to someone locked in a fairytale in which she is rescued and taken care of. In retrospect, it's obvious a female clinician would have served her better. I was unwilling to accept her emotional immaturity and meet her where she was, because I could not accept where she was. Every time she came to session in low cut blouses and short skirts, I strengthened my resolve to prove that not all men would treat her as an object or welcome her advances. The struggle with her unwillingness to accept boundaries was as much my issue as hers.

These difficulties in the early years of my practice were symptomatic of a problem with the larger therapeutic culture: in many outpatient clinics, specializing according to aptitude or preference is never an option. You take who is referred to you because agencies value money over the well-being of clients and clinicians. And that's that. So in my case, you had a clinician with no aptitude for serving those with personality disorders doing exactly that. No one wins, no one gets better.

We work so hard to understand others and so little to understand ourselves. We seek to be highly skilled and knowledgeable but not to be healthy. We focus on our performance rather than our being. It takes a lot of vulnerability to admit we're not good at aspects of our professions. I've seen very little in the field that meaningfully encouraged me to do the very things I want my clients to do.

How about you?

- We ask them to be vulnerable. What's your comfort level with vulnerability?
- We ask them to trust us. Take stock: How fully do you doubt or trust yourself?
- We urge them to engage in self-care, maintain excellent nutrition, exercise, get enough sleep, hydrate, journal, take vacations, develop natural supports, cultivate intimate connections. Take a quick personal inventory on those
- We want them to pursue the career path they most want. Is that the one you're on?
- We know where their dating relationships and partnerships are headed. How about yours?
- We spot their burn out a mile away. How close are you?

- We believe they will benefit from therapy. Maybe it's time for you to have some too?

Chill the Fuck Out

Once, a mentor asked me to guess how old I'd be when my first heart attack arrived. I reacted, predictably, with defensiveness. Sure, I was very busy, arguably too busy, but I was doing Very Important Things. I was fine. I didn't need help, didn't need to slow down, and no one was having a heart attack anytime soon.

My mentor scoffed, and told me a bit about AA folklore.

In the earliest days of AA, lots of suggestions were offered regarding rules members should adhere to. Ultimately, they were all thrown out in favor of the twelve steps and traditions, and the ethic of each AA group being sovereign and self-governing. My mentor explained that of all the proposed rules from back in the day, only one remained. She thought I would benefit from this "rule number 62."

I was excited, and asked her what it was.

"Don't take yourself so damn seriously."

Too often we work ourselves into exhaustion and burnout, wait until we can't do it all anymore, and then quit. It's far better to take stock regularly of both the external and internal. Examining the expectations and standards we hold ourselves to, and considering whether they're realistic, affords us opportunities to take the weight of the world off our shoulders.

It also makes clear who the fucker is that keeps loading on the weight.

It's long been part of our social vernacular to tell folks to "lighten up," but how do you actually do that? I suggest starting with the mundane and obvious. Is there one responsibility you're willing to part with? Is there a chore or recurring task you can hire someone to do? Ideally, is there something you really hate doing, something that has to get done that you can delegate to someone else? In my case, one of those things is yard work. It took years of misery before I realized that not only am I terrible at it, but I detest doing it. Becoming successful as a therapist allowed me to pay someone else to handle tasks that I erroneously associated with being independent and self-sufficient.

If you're like me, then you have unhealthy expectations of independence and autonomy based in blue-collar roots and/or a Puritan work ethic. These expectations have nothing to do with what we love, nor are they supportive of our true passions; indeed, they often get in the way of what we really want to be doing. The simplest way to lighten up: Do more of what you love and less of what you don't. I can do one extra hour of therapy and afford eight hours of house cleaning services. Consider that ratio before you vacuum again.

There's something deeper at work here, too: most of us never really consider how important it actually is for these mundane tasks to get done. Why do you mow the lawn so obsessively? Does the length of your grass truly matter to you? Do you need to be the one who mows it? Is it cost effective for you to do it yourself?

Then there's the bigger and more difficult form of lightening up that requires introspection. The hardest part of this is that success hinges on rigorous honesty with self, coupled with a willingness to allow ourselves to be served. It's as simple as asking ourselves, "What still hurts?" We often find that we continue to carry resentments (past pain and anger) as well as both shame and guilt that don't truly belong to us.

Lightening up means examining the reasons we see ourselves as insufficient/not good enough. Our attempts to be more and do more are usually attempts to fill the emptiness and cover up our insecurities. What keeps you from feeling enough? Whose approval do you most crave? Here's a crazy idea: Maybe the approval you most need is your own?

Let's lighten your load:
- What are the mundane chores you can eliminate from your life?
- Does your lifestyle fully support your values?

- What do you feel trapped by? Finances? Responsibilities? Other people's expectations?
- How can you become free of those?
- Who do you know in similar straits? Can you support one another in making changes?
- What still hurts?
- What prevents you from being proud of you?
- Who are you trying to impress? Why? What's the cost and benefit of that?

Fuck Professionalism

Professionalism is a meaningless term applied to a vaguely defined set of unspoken expectations that are more geared toward protecting liability than promoting anyone's well-being. It costs too much. It's inauthentic and inhibiting. There are a handful of ideas in the entirety of what we call professionalism that matter, nearly all of which are matters of common sense and not being an asshole: Show up on time, do your job as well as you can do it, help others.

When my kids were in elementary school, they were occasionally admonished by teachers who advised that their behavior was not "appropriate." (My wife and I did our kids the dubious service of teaching them sarcasm at very young ages). "Appropriate" implies a uniform, agreed upon standard that's widely understood and accessible. In much the same way, we espouse "professionalism." There is variance from one field to another, but on the whole, being "professional" in the healing and helping professions can be translated to, "Present a high-quality persona and make sure you appear completely composed and in control in all of your affairs." In other words, be full of shit.

This should be obvious by now, but I'll take authenticity over professionalism any day. Professionalism in the healing and helping fields is restrictive. It dictates empathy from women and authoritarianism from men. It perpetuates not only traditional gender roles but all of our other isms as well. It's evident in realities like the fact that in social work women vastly outnumber men, yet men hold the majority of top management positions.

Professionalism is homogeneous. It's a half-assed operationalization of our codes of ethics, workplace policies and procedures, state and federal regulations and funding source requirements all rolled up into a poorly communicated set of expectations. You're supposed to know all of this even though nobody told you much about it. You're also supposed to understand that while these apply in the workplace, they often will not after hours, while out of town on seminars, or at holiday office parties.

You're expected to know how professionalism has specific variances in your place of employment by virtue of your status, gender, age, race, sexual orientation and a myriad of other factors, none of which will ever be overtly expressed. This is how isms work – they create unrealistic and unspoken expectations and biases. We who see ourselves as free-thinking and socially aware tend to oppress our own. Self-expression and individualism are not supported, and are, in fact, actively discouraged.

Professionalism, as a concept, is in no way applicable to how we relate to ourselves, only in how we regulate and present ourselves. It's sterile, based on a false neutrality, and full of contradictions that favor our employer over ourselves and our clients: Be interesting but not provocative. Be engaging but not intrusive. Confront problems but avoid conflict. Be effective but always remain in the parameters of what we are comfortable with. We are assigned boundaries - not free to choose them. This is no coincidence. Professionalism comes disguised as the mode of conduct that best supports our mission, but in fact its only purpose is to protect our organizations from liability, without concern for individual needs or, more importantly, the quality of service we provide our clients.

The intimate nature of our work is minimalized and set aside in the context of professionalism. It certainly would never be considered professional to cry, scream, or emote in anything other than a highly controlled manner regardless of what we're experiencing. We who make our living in other people's pain are expected to remain unmoved and in control at all times.

Do excellent work. Do it with a great bedside manner but without loss of composure. Do it with empathy but ignore that our capacity for empathy is based on personal, painful experiences. Use your time with your supervisor for administrative tasks and case reviews, not examining and working on your own state of being. Be stoic. Do not express compassion fatigue or burnout, but by all means go home and drink yourself silly.

"Hey, welcome to our agency! We're a family here!"

My agency is a family, too, but one that's based in love and choice, not in dysfunctional dynamics. My folks are encouraged to take risks and leave concern about liability to me.

The simple truth is that our work is done one-on-one, behind closed doors. As such, there's no way to protect yourself from liability. All you have is your integrity and honorable intentions. Concern for covering your own ass will detract from serving the client. That's why I tell my employees, "I'm going to have your back, even when you're wrong."

I hope you get to work for exceptionally supportive people, or that you create your own such practice. In the meantime:

- Have you meaningfully considered the norms of your organization and how "professionalism" is defined?

- How safe is it to lose composure when clients are not present?
- How could you and your colleagues be more supportive of one another? What prevents that?
- Whose definitions are you living by? Who have you emulated? Is it how you truly want to be?

So Many Pitfalls, so Little Time

I have a shiny new intern. She has that fresh, just started the second year of grad school smell. She's adorably dorky and endearingly anxious. She's very bright and super analytical, incredibly well read and studies the way I used to – in the belief that if you learn enough, you won't be afraid. She hears me saying it's normal to be scared and that all of us were early on. In that moment, I become not only the clinical supervisor she's dreamed of but also the dad she always wished she had. Ideally, we all would have had parents who reassured us, normalized our emotional experiences, and nurtured our growth. Too few of us had that, and so those who offer it are likely to be seen as idealized parent figures. I become "dad" when I give what other men failed to.

She wants to get off to a solid start and make good first impressions.

I want her to relax, settle the fuck down, and get comfortable in her own skin.

I'm urging her to forgo her intellect and favor her intuition. I don't need to remind myself how hard that is to hear, because it shows on her face. We do what we're comfortable doing. To have someone we respect suggest that we need to change means:

- They've seen through our persona, which leaves us feeling exposed
- They're offering a viable alternative that we're not comfortable with, because we favor the appearance of confidence over admitting we don't know things
- We're left in the vulnerable position of being taught and the terrifying position of being accountable for utilizing what we learn.
- While we may be comfortable failing ourselves, we must reconcile that developing better tools means we provide better service (Feeling afraid and compelled out of our comfort zones simultaneously).

It's not like I've forgotten what it felt like to be in her shoes. It just takes me a minute to access what I've overcome because I don't think about it until I'm looking at it through her eyes. I recall the incredible stress I experienced in trying to maintain my composure in those early years.
Only in retrospect could I see how hard I tried to fool my supervisors and myself into believing that I knew what I was doing and furthermore, felt confident about it. Serving others ought to come with a list of health and practical expectations. In grad school they made me feel I should be able to serve

greatly and autonomously. I didn't know what my limitations were, and no one told me that it was okay to have them.

I'm your therapist. I have the answers to every question. I can help with any problem. I don't yet know you, but I care deeply about you. Just tell me what you need, and we'll have a healthy nonreciprocal relationship.

It's laughable. Why did I have such unrealistic standards and such unhealthy coping? Because scared and scarred have a reciprocal relationship. I hid both. It's all a setup, a closed circuit—fear begets scarring, scarring begets fear--but you don't know that until you can't hide your scars anymore.

Franklin Roosevelt said, "The only thing we have to fear is fear itself." Roosevelt was known to be a huge fan of Henry David Thoreau. I and many others believe he was bastardizing a line Thoreau journaled, "Nothing is so much to be feared as fear."

Go to Youtube right now and listen to Pop Evil sing, "Waking Lions." How we deal with fear determines the lion's share of what's possible in our lives. Being alone with fear is a recipe for disaster. Do you want to be a great leader? Tell everyone your fears and then enlist their help in overcoming them.

I tell my intern obvious things because she's overlooked them. That's what fear does—distracts you, blinds you, makes you miss things. How we cope with it determines what is possible in our lives. She's been conditioned to hide all of her "negative" emotions. She's a frustrated chameleon because in my office, her camouflage no longer works.

Deep down we all believe that we're uniquely fucked up in ways that no one else is or could possibly understand. That's the essence of shame. It leaves us isolated in false beliefs and so hidden that we lose ourselves in its darkness.

Clinical supervision is like parenting – you want to teach your children every lesson you've ever learned to spare them pain. In both cases, it's righteous. It doesn't work in raising adolescents and young adults. It can work in supervision because you're not their parent – you're usually the parent they should have had. You're both symbolically and practically authoritative and therefore loved, rebelled against, sought after, feared, appreciated, and powerful.

Well into my career, I learned how to use countertransference and transference as tools with clients. Later I learned positive manipulation with my supervisees. When I got good at those things, I stopped thinking about them. If one is not careful, it becomes a way of being. Then you're gradually everyone's mom or dad (whether you're working or not).

People do what they have the most familiarity and confidence in doing. I'm no different, and so it's a rare person that I'm not subconsciously parenting. See the scars, trace the origins of the scars. Teach them how to heal the scars. See the unmet need, meet the need. Believe in them until they believe in themselves. It's a mixed bag. Investing in others brings us great joy, but the pitfall is that it can easily be one more way in which we distract ourselves from ourselves.

To live the life of a healer (and it is a lifestyle; let's get rid of the idea that this is a 9-to-5 gig) you have to keep growing and connecting. Every time I become complacent or am not sufficiently mindful, I find myself in a new and terrible situation that could have been avoided.

The best practical advice I've ever heard: "Keep your head where your feet are at."

And so I will teach my young intern that she is a very lovely hypocrite, in her desire to facilitate what she has not yet experienced. She got in for what felt like all the right reasons, and unless we have a hundred "Come to Jesus" talks, she'll learn everything the hard way--assuming she doesn't burn out first.

Take stock:

- Look back on your start in the field. How did you deal with fear at that time? How do you deal with it now?
- Regardless of whether you're new or seasoned, have you meaningfully considered the value of what you've learned and sought opportunities to teach it to others?
- Are you willing to share your mistakes that others might learn from them?
- What have you yet to overcome in your current professional role?
- How has your profession impacted your lifestyle? What changes are you glad for? Which do you need to undo?

Call a Spade a Fucking Spade

I had a fascinating conversation with a colleague who also happens to be a client recently. She asked, "Do you ever feel like you should be a little less honest?" I laughed wickedly because I know myself well. I can be scathing. My approach is a steel-toed boot followed by hugs and affirmation. ("You're fucked, but I believe in you and will help you get better.") I acknowledged that, being overzealous by nature, many times I have doled out too much truth in one sitting, sure. But too much of a good thing doesn't somehow make that good thing bad. And I have never regretted being brutally candid and forthcoming as to what I think the truth is.

I do not profess that my truth is the truth. I trust what I sense intuitively, and I follow it into some pretty dark places. There's a reason why I'm only interested in serving folks who have been through hell and shown incredible resilience. They're the ones with the guts to change their lives and overcome what they survived.

Subtlety is lost on people like us. Half-truths and kid gloves don't work. Pulling punches is a waste of time. Plenty of therapists will listen compassionately and assure you that you're a good person and that people like you. Those therapists are the stereotype of my profession, and deservedly so. They're usually middle-aged women who wear big, clunky jewelry. They rock Birkenstocks, pastels, flowing skirts, and usually have impossibly frizzy hair. They often own a herd of cats, and make frequent visits to their gastroenterologist because anxiety has worn holes in their insides. These are people who tend to be terrified of my tribe, because they're just intuitive enough to know that we can see what they hide.

There's nothing wrong with a client wanting someone who will listen and affirm, but don't think for one minute that it's going to result in transforming a life.

Some folks need garden variety therapy. They're healthy people, and they have a good life. Let's say they're 45 and their mom dies. A year later, they find themselves stuck in their grief and are struggling to adjust to life without mom. For these folks, the stereotypical therapist can be very helpful. They'll hand out tissues, offer reassurance, and explain the stages of grief. This is worthwhile and important work—it's just not my jam. I find that work too easy and therefore dull.

The work I crave is trying to bring light into the darkest of places. In the absence of light, it's tough for folks to know when they're lying to themselves. I work to find the contradictions. I seek the false belief that was internalized and expose it. Confront it. Take risks. Other approaches might be ok; they're just not all that satisfying because they're not apt to meaningfully challenge the client or the practitioner.

How about you:
- What do you most need to be challenged on?
- What are the white lies you tend to tell yourself?
- How challenging is your current work?
- Be rigorously honest with yourself – are you challenged? Overwhelmed? Bored?
- What do you most want to learn or get better at doing?

We're Not Fucking Experts

An accurate, honest description of the job we do would scare away all but the truly masochistic. When I tell my bachelor-level students about all the unhealthiness that I have seen and experienced in the healing and helping professions, they sigh and seem to think, "You poor man, you've become old, cynical and bitter. What you're saying can't possibly be true."

What I tell them is what I wish I'd been told before I entered the field. What you are setting out to do is well intended but too often misguided. You believe that you are entering the field for completely healthy reasons. Are you subconsciously hoping that helping others will heal you? (Spoiler alert: It won't).

I hope to get them (for the first time in a very long time, if ever) to look at themselves the way they will be looking at patients/clients. Why do you do what you do? What drives you? What fucks you up? What's the emptiness in you? What do you need?

What do you believe is going to make you successful professionally? Will it be mastery of technique or a thorough understanding of theories? Will you become an expert in multiple approaches that are backed by very impressive research? That's what I set out to do too. In retrospect, I see my illusions. I wanted to believe that if I knew enough, worked hard enough and most importantly, sacrificed enough, I'd no longer be afraid and be excellent in my professional role.

I have not facilitated growth and healing by mastering Cognitive Behavioral Therapy. I left grad school with what I thought was a tool box full of incredibly effective interventions. What I discovered was that relating to people based on theoretical approaches and preconceived strategies is a fool's errand.

Fortunately, I got a heads-up early on that it might not work well. I had learned about active listening skills and reframing in class. I came home to an intense conversation with my wife that night. I decided to check in with her. I tried reflecting, "What I hear you saying is…" That's as far as I got. She glared at me and yelled, "I just fucking told you what you *heard me saying.* You can do that shit at work, but don't you dare do it with me."

It turned out that talking that way in my early days as a therapist was never well received. It elicited a lot of eye rolls and folks checking out. The simple truth is that no one other than stereotypical social workers talk like that. Using language that is less than genuine creates distance where we're trying to foster intimate connections. Keep it simple – don't talk like anyone else. Be real, be completely in the moment, and say whatever you say in your own voice.

I see the best work I have done as a byproduct of my willingness to muddle. I'm able and willing to be fully present when I have no idea what to do next. My tolerance for uncertainty and working in true collaboration with my clients—making it up as we go along, in other words—has made a great deal possible.

What truly set me free was the idea that **you don't always have to know what to do.** This is why the whole concept of being an expert is distasteful to me – experts are always supposed to know what to do and how to do it optimally. In that perspective, the client is a passive recipient of brilliance and flourishes by what the professional does.

That concept works to a limited extent in the medical model because it involves objective problems that have clear solutions. If you have a broken leg, you can see ten different doctors, all of whom will come to the same diagnosis, provide the same treatment, and the same prognosis.

In mental health, we're making it up as we go along. The same patient could see ten clinicians, get ten different diagnoses, ten different forms of treatment prescribed and get ten different prognoses. The overlap of symptoms between disorders alone causes this. Then add in the variety of perspectives based on training. Now muddy the waters by factoring how our personal experiences impact our professional perspectives.

It all comes back to the succinct brilliance of Anais Nin: "We see things not as they are, but as we are."

So, I don't want to be an expert. I seek to be a guide because while I have not been a part of your journey, I have walked similar terrain myself, and with many others.
I want to be a mirror and a confidant. I want to be someone who challenges and above all, I want to be a cheerleader who applauds every effort to get better. In this way, I can maintain a mix of humility and excellent service.

And you?

- What's your willingness to muddle?
- How comfortable are you in simply being fully present in the moment?
- Is there perhaps something lacking in your acceptance of self that would make you more confident in serving others?
- How important is it to you to be seen in a particular light by those you serve? How much control do you have over that?

Counseling and Relationships

There are many things my clients have a right to know about me. Amusingly, they often find it hard to ask very basic questions. Most every set of partners I've served as a couple's counselor have awkwardly steeled themselves to ask about my relational history. This is a very good idea. Who wants to see a relationship counselor who's been divorced three times?

I'm blessed to be an old married guy. We've been together over 30 years. My wife finds it alternately laughable and annoying that there are a host of things I don't pay attention to in life. Problematically, it doesn't really register when people are flirting with me. Unless it's a client, I'll often miss it because frankly, I'm not looking for it and I find it tedious. There's a wedding ring in the customary place, and if you've known me for more than five minutes, it should be obvious that I'm excessively loyal and not a person who has affairs.

For all that I can say about partnerships and marriage, I most often quote my wife the accountant: "Relationships are work. You either work together in an ongoing fashion, addressing all the tough stuff, or you get to have an unsatisfying relationship." It's that simple.

In the movie Last Vegas, Kevin Kline turns down the opportunity to have an affair he knows would involve outstanding sex by explaining that anything potentially wonderful can only be and remain such when it can be shared with his wife.

I hope you get to have what I have. If you don't yet, I'll let you in on what I tell most couples when I'm asked why so many marriages and partnerships fail, "Two people who don't especially like themselves try to love each other." For healers and helpers, "don't especially like" can be replaced with "ambivalent toward self" or even, "filled with self-loathing."

I have found that there are two foundational relationships for all others: the one I have with me and the one I have with my Higher Power. I've learned that spirituality works a lot like my marriage does. When I'm not good to me, I distance myself from my wife emotionally. In the same fashion, when I'm not treating me well, the Universe doesn't hear from me for a while.

In the throes of being my own worst enemy, the best I could be was a codependent, unhealthy partner who didn't practice reciprocity at all. Believing myself to be unworthy meant constantly earning love from a person who wanted to give it unconditionally.

The principal reason I have a successful marriage today is because my wife did not kill me in our early years, though she would have been justified in doing so.

Right around our two-year anniversary, we had a fight that culminated in her screaming at me, "You are not solely responsible for my happiness." To which I offered a bewildered look. In retrospect, I see that she alone is responsible for her happiness. I get to add to it, but when I tried to take responsibility for it, I was largely avoiding the responsibilities I have for my own needs and feelings.

When you grow up in an unhealthy family, you learn all the wrong things. I didn't learn to <u>care for</u>; I learned to <u>take care of</u>. When you're not taught that you're worthy; you don't come to value yourself. Two problems: We don't nurture or protect what we do not value, and we come to resent the responsibilities we take on for others' wants, needs, and feelings, conveniently overlooking the fact that they didn't ask us to.

The day of reckoning came when I noticed how much I resented the expectations of those closest to me. In exasperation, I asked my wife, "Why does everyone we know believe that I can move mountains singlehandedly?" She laughed wickedly and asked, "Have you met you? That's what you do."

Whatever we repeatedly do will very naturally come to be expected of us. What I did was unhealthy, but I did it consistently and with neither complaint nor request for help. I did not tolerate help, support, or encouragement. When others offered, I refused. When they complimented, praised, or offered me recognition, I responded as I would to a server who's bringing me a dish after I'm already stuffed, "No, thank you. Take that away. I'm already uncomfortable, and you're adding to it."

We can't teach what we haven't both learned and lived. If our partnerships aren't healthy, we'll likely find it difficult to facilitate growth amongst partners.
If we fear intimacy, we can't nurture it among others and worse, we'll struggle to maintain neutrality in working with couples and families. We will be at risk of identifying with one party and susceptible to siding with those who struggle in similar fashions to ourselves.

Spotting transference and countertransference gets tougher as we add people to the room. What remains constant is that the most important person for you to understand, attend to, and be present with is you. The work you do will likely magnify your personal life. If you serve those who go without basic life needs, you will find yourself grateful that your needs are met. If you serve those who struggle in parenting, partnering, or in relating to their families of origin, you will find yourself reevaluating those relationships in your own life.

Potentially uncomfortable questions:

- So, now that we're talking about it, what is that quality of your partnership or single life?
- Friendships? Relations with family?
- What's missing? What needs to change?
- How can your needs be more fully met?
- What's your willingness to ask for what you most want?

We're Full of Shit

I put two curses on every clinician I supervise. The first is that I hope they fail epically. This is, for obvious reasons, not well-received. I go on to explain that when we don't fail that means we didn't risk enough—the bar was not set sufficiently high. Failure instructs, so long as we're open to learning from it. What's more, your clients will forgive you when you fail, because they'll see that you're willing to go to any lengths to promote their recovery. Which is only fair, considering that's exactly what we ask of them.

The second curse I put on my clinicians is: I hope you have a hundred clients just like you. And my employees marvel at how often they do receive clients that they have a lot in common with. I tell them this is a gift from the Universe, that they may learn about themselves by serving folks they identify with and relate to. But this is often painful. It triggers our own stuff, but more profoundly, we find ourselves having to empathize with someone who is very similar to the person we've been ignoring. All roads lead back to self.

The greatest piece of advice I give to employees is to follow their intuition. It's immeasurably frustrating to those I've supervised how often I'll respond to a question by asking, "What does your gut say?" The desire for direction is strong, and it increases proportionately to our fears. Intuition trumps intellect, but fear overshadows both. I urge folks to practice separating what they know in their heads, feel in their hearts, and sense from their guts. Getting on the same page with ourselves makes our work vastly more manageable.

Here's an all-purpose tool: What is the thing you most fear occurring? Examine it. Why are you afraid of it? What's the worst that can happen? It's common for healers and helpers to avoid conflict and confrontation. Our fear of these experiences leads us to unwittingly imposing limits on our approach, whereas tolerating risk leads us toward creative solutions.

Early in my career, my greatest fear was being fired by a client and having to explain to an employer why I'd lost them revenue. Unfortunately, I was often faced with folks who just weren't ready and willing to change. This was especially true of the high functioning addicts and alcoholics I treated.

My mentor for addictions counseling explained, "If you're not making an alcoholic or addict angry on a fairly regular basis then you're probably not helping them. Early on, they call me a bitch because I point out painful truths, but if they're ready and willing, they'll keep coming back." I've since learned that the greatest service I can provide to those in active addiction or early recovery is to confront self-deception and speak the truth in no uncertain terms.

It took me a long time to get good at it. At first, I spoke things directly but with excessive sensitivity. When you're telling folks things they don't want to hear, they tend to deflect such statements subconsciously. Today I say things like, "You're full of shit." That's a hard statement to dismiss. It's a risk, but it tends to create opportunities.

Confrontation will almost inevitably result in your client either temporarily checking out or (more often) becoming angry and defensive. Stay the course. Damned few people immediately appreciate being called out on their bullshit, but they'll thank you for it later. It's the acronym for DENIAL – Don't Even kNow When I'm Lying (to Myself). It's a huge part of how addiction and other forms of self-destruction strip away a person's identity, character, beliefs, and values. It's easy to understand why these clients become angry when confronted with the truth—they've spent so long convincing themselves of their own lies. What else do we expect, if not confrontation and fury, when someone refuses to play along?

I met Matthew just as I was getting good at confrontation. He was a brilliant and well-loved school teacher. He would allude vaguely to his, "drinking issue." I countered that everyone has issues, but he seemed to have the whole subscription. He left treatment because I pointed out a fifth of vodka a day was neither sustainable nor manageable. He departed after explaining that I was crass and abrasive.

The unexpected twist was that Matthew came back again and again over many years. He would only engage in a few sessions before he'd stop showing up, but he would always return. I adjusted accordingly. Each time he came in, I focused on planting just a few seeds and nurturing their growth. The last time he came back, he stayed for almost two years. Today he's been sober and fully living for many years.

Matthew knew that what offended him was the truth. He kept returning to me because he knew that unlike everyone else in his life, he couldn't bullshit me. If I had relied on intellect and taken his narratives at face value, I'd have never known there was a serious problem. I pushed and pushed because my gut told me that a "few drinks a night" was a sugar-coated version of the truth.

(in my best M.C. Hammer voice) It's journal time!

1. Describe to me the client you've had/will have that is just like you. What are they struggling with?
2. The next time you face this, will you own your hypocrisy?
3. What is your resolve? From today forward, when you catch yourself giving advice that you don't take, what will you do? (Not for the client – for you)

4. What are you trying not to know?

Fear is a Four Letter Word

My understanding of how to effectively treat trauma was so lacking early on that I believed it possible to avoid triggering my clients in session. This delusion came crashing down years ago one afternoon in May. Barbra walked across the parking lot smiling and laughing, but in my office almost immediately dissociated—checked out mentally and shut down emotionally. She was to amenable to my suggestions, too pliable. She wasn't really there. She gave brief and rote answers to my questions about her day, her health, and her progress. It's disconcerting to talk with folks who have enormous experience functioning while checked out. Her eyes were glazed over, and her affect was flat. I asked if she'd like to go to Mars with me. She immediately answered that would be fine.

Nowhere in my training was I taught how to effectively deal with this. I learned how to deal with it from countless of hours of sitting with folks who appear to be present but aren't. In my search for solutions, I moved away from western medicine and found enormous benefit in different forms of mindfulness exercises, meditation, and bodywork.

With Barbara, I used the five senses to connect her back to the here and now. I walked her through some breathing exercises and steps to release muscle tension (to counteract her fight or flight response). Processing after she returned to the present, she was able to tell me—and realize for herself—that the smell of lilacs outside in the parking lot had connected her to a horrific memory.

Even once I understood far more about how to do trauma work, I was still completely fucked up about it. I was afraid of triggering my clients and sought control over where sessions would go. Instead of treating them, I wanted to protect them. I felt personally responsible for their emotive state and overall well-being. What could be more codependent? I experienced this even as I was teaching my clients that they were not responsible for the feelings of others. Blind spots: we've all got 'em, even the supposedly omnipotent and flawless therapist.

The overwhelming majority of my clients were women, and I came to understand that in many respects, I related to them largely as I did my mother. This was part of the problem. Therapy is a non-reciprocal relationship that's centered upon meeting the needs of a vulnerable person. I was taught to relate that way in my family of origin and had yet to outgrow it.

The part of my brain that spots my well-intended hypocrisy kept lighting up like a Christmas tree. I brought my concerns to a colleague who was both patient and sarcastic. "How good of you to protect us women from ourselves!

Without your benevolence, we'd have to experience our own pain and create our own solutions!" My friend dropped a lot of very loving anvils upon my head. She knows that just like the folks I serve, subtlety is the worst possible means to point me toward acceptance and change.

- What's your weakness?
- What are the hardest things for you to do professionally?
- How do those connect to your past and present?
- We all have architypes for how we relate to others. Tell me about yours.

It Doesn't Matter What You Want

Recently one of my clinicians asked, "When is it ok to simply acknowledge that therapy isn't helping and stop?" This question was painful for him because his client is an adolescent who shows every sign of being sociopathic. There are few clinical situations in which progress, no matter how incremental, could feel so urgent, and in which failure has such potential to affect the therapist's emotional well-being.

My heart went out to him. We both have children older than this client. What the clinician is faced with is something he sees as an unacceptable truth. To the core of his being, that he cannot instill a conscience within his client is intolerable. It is extremely difficult to treat a child in therapy and not care and feel protective of them on nearly the same level as you do your children. Failure can be crushing.

The most painful thing I've ever seen is the vacant expression in the eyes of a child who simply broke. I once worked with a boy who had burned through twenty-six foster homes in three years. I can still picture his dark brown eyes and the ambivalence within them. No hope. No expectations. Nothing existed for him beyond the present moment.

"Jack" was intelligent and endlessly curious about how machines of every type operated. He enjoyed sports, video games, and climbing trees. He craved attention from maternal women.

He would do things that every medical journal in the world says a human being cannot do. He seemed to experience no physical sensations of any kind. Like many survivors of sexual trauma, a bowel movement triggered his memories of past abuse. He would go weeks at a time without having them. The break between his body, mind, and spirit seemed irreparable, and it devastated me.

I had a son his age at the time. I wanted a way to carve out a piece of my heart and transplant it into him. I was furious at the man who raped the boy countless times and self-righteously angry with the system that failed him over and over again.

And none of that anger helped the boy one damned bit. It just ate away at me.

The tremendous, counterintuitive benefit of accepting the unacceptable is that we're then free to focus fully on what we can do. Once I stopped trying to get the kid to care, I was free to teach him how to be more adaptive and how to be more responsive and less reactive. There were plenty of things he was willing to learn – they just weren't the ones I wanted for him. Once I realized that what I wanted didn't matter a bit, I was able to help him.

That's one of the toughest lessons in doing trauma work – sometimes it couldn't be less relevant what you want for your client. Believe in them. Care about them. Work hard for them. Accept the adage that you can bring a horse to water, but you can't make it drink. Just do what you can. I remind my clinicians that very often it's not what we do that really makes a difference. It's who we are, and by being the best possible version of our authentic selves, we prove that some who believe they are broken not only recover, but flourish.

I wish I could tell you Jack's story ended happily, but the truth is I don't know. Part of my unhealthy coping at the time was using "inappropriate" humor with coworkers. This became an excuse for my employer to fire me (after turning down my resignation), and I was not allowed even to say goodbye to Jack. Last I knew, he was in juvenile detention. Unacceptable outcomes are sometimes part of our work, and we must accept and deal with them. The only thing that's up for grabs is whether we cope in healthy ways.

How about you?
- What's the most unacceptable aspect of your work?
- What will you do to accept it?
- How many barriers are you willing to have to your serenity?

- How can you express the righteous anger you incur professionally in order to release it?

Dare Greatly

Most of us are actors and actresses who embrace the parts we're comfortable and familiar fulfilling. We do this very naturally and subconsciously by remaining in the roles assigned by our families of origin. If you're not sure about that, pay close attention the next time you go home for the holidays. Do you dread going? Do they relate to you based on who you are or who they believe you to be? Do you behave differently among family?

Some of us were taught to be caregivers and others to be peacekeepers. Some of us were designated as "the smart one," "the pretty one," or "the hard worker." The development of a child is guided largely by what they're told about themselves. Teach a child their worth and place in the world, and they will generally believe you. Teach them they have no worth and no place, and they'll buy that, too.

To break out of the molds we were cast in is a very rare thing indeed. The simple truth is that most people never make fundamental changes in their way of being nor in how they relate to themselves and others. Where we live, who we marry, our careers, how we raise our children—all these things are based on the standards and expectations of our families. The most ready example of this is nurses – more so than any profession, nurses are likely to have grown up in families where alcoholism/addiction was present.

It makes sense. You grow up taking care of others and dealing with unreasonable people, so as an adult you do it for a living. There's always a reason why people pick healing and helping professions. What's astounding is how often we're unaware of our true motives. We don't "want to help people." We're acting out behavioral themes that were set long before we had any idea what we wanted to do with our professional lives.

If the average nurse is honest, they'll tell you some horror stories about what's normative regarding how they relate to one another professionally. The prevailing adage is that they "eat their young." The parallel to an abusive family of origin is clear: it wasn't safe to direct our negative emotions towards our parents (doctors and administrators), so we take it out on our siblings (other nurses).

More so than any profession, nurses have been absolutely paranoid about their confidentiality in treatment with me. I most often saw them after hours when the waiting room was empty, and my staff had gone home. Anxiety, addiction, and extremely abusive/unhealthy relationships (often all three) were the most common reasons for seeking help. When I'd ask a nurse to consider that their lives can be appreciably better, they'd usually see it as akin to me asking a fish to consider learning to fly.

It's not that we can't, it's that we're afraid to imagine we can. We look at our professions as defining who we are, and so asking someone to conceptualize a better life is akin to asking them to go into an entirely different field, one in which they have no experience and cannot conceive of learning how to do. The emotional response is, "But I've already invested so much in this one!" Yes, that's true. How has your investment paid off?

The struggle for us is that our jobs are our identity. We live in a culture within which one of the first things you're asked upon meeting someone for the first time is, "What do you do?" Folks will attach expectations and assumptions accordingly. If we were to answer the question with something other than a career label, it's unlikely we'd be taken seriously. And herein lies the problem. If we were to ask the question, and answer it, with something other than our jobs in mind, that would likely give a lot more insight into who we are.

What do I do? Thanks for asking. I self-actualize, pray, and fall asleep whenever I meditate too long. I play poker in seedy underground games. I'm an avid fan of music. I write blogs. I laugh loudly and often. I like weird people, and I like nothing more than spending hours talking with them. I teach by example. I facilitate growth and healing. I'm an aspiring author. I'm a walking, talking, breathing set of contradictions, and a seriously fucked up individual who's consistently getting better.

What the fuck do you do? By which I mean: who and how are you when you're not working?

What we're really asking in "What do you do" is, "How do you do to exchange your time, talents, and efforts for money?" If the answer is, "I'm a prostitute," then come sit by me.
If the answer is "I work for the IRS," you're going to have to come up with something vastly more interesting to get my attention.

But then, if what you do when you're not working is keep a meticulous house, fret over your financial investments, or fuck somebody else's spouse (without pay), then chances are, you're not living an authentic life or achieving the quality of life you truly want. Conforming to social norms and values is disingenuous, and it makes you far less appealing, at least to me. More importantly, it makes you less effective in your service to others.

What do you wish you could tell people about yourself? When asked what you do, why do you respond by saying "I'm a therapist," instead of saying, "I sleep in the nude and sing karaoke every Tuesday night"? What's keeping you from telling people who you are, rather than how you make money?

Define yourself for yourself and then worry about how you'll describe it to others (or don't, because fuck 'em; you don't have to explain anything). My challenge to you is to identify strengths you possess that are not simply descriptions of how you are to others: kind, compassionate, honest, a good friend, loyal, loving, accepting. Give me the stuff that's just yours: Smart, talented, insightful, wise, creative, tenacious, resilient. What positives dare you incorporate into your definition? What's the contrast between how you see you and how others do? (Your false beliefs, excessive criticism of self, impossible societal standards and excessive humility). What's the contrast between how your colleagues and friends see you and how your family of origin sees you (the healthy among the former sees you, the latter focuses on how you're not who/how they most want you to be).

The devil isn't in the details. The bastard hides in the conflicts and contradictions. Mental illness and addiction have a way better shot of manifesting and flourishing within those of us who deflect praise and recognition. Stop saying, "It's nothing." Start taking it in. Better yet, start writing it down. A dear friend of mine had made amazing gains through the course of her recovery from addiction, yet she continued to play small and stay with the familiar. Her sponsor was as old school as they come, and, having lost patience, demanded that she keep a notebook and at the end of each day, write down every bit of praise and recognition received.

My friend did as instructed, and over time accumulated a great deal of evidence that she was selling herself short in her own mind. The world saw her as much better than she did, but this wouldn't sink in for her until she had the evidence right there in black and white on the pages in front of her.

Try to notice how readily you dismiss the gifts others give you. The way I see it, those you serve not only have every right to speak well of you, but you also have a responsibility to honor their truth. More contrast – we define ourselves by our professions but dismiss the opinions of those we serve. We never consciously do this. We do it subconsciously because it's a departure from the self-image we're given and maintain.

The truth is – accepting outside input will change you. We fight to stay in our tiny little comfort zones because we're afraid to be powerful, afraid to be thought well of and it's all because of the bullshit idea that if we accept what they already see, then we'll fall from grace. The pressure to not disappoint is crippling but it's based on the idea that everything is conditional, and everyone's expectations are within our control.

Say that shit out loud. "If I accept that they think so highly of me, I will let them down, and then they'll realize that I'm not really that good. Now imagine saying it to them, "If I see myself as you do, I'll fuck everything up and then you won't think well of me anymore." Logically, this would mean the surest way to maintain others having a positive view of us is to deny ourselves that right. Fuck that.

When I process these types of fear with my clients; they almost inevitably express fears of becoming arrogant or grandiose. We can only conceive of change as a process of moving very quickly from one extreme to the other. So, if we are overly humble or ashamed, it follows that we fear becoming insufferably impressed with ourselves.

The greatest benefits of accountability and letting people really know us is that we get to skip the exhaustive processes of endlessly monitoring and evaluating ourselves. We can seek feedback and input from others. We can share what we fear doing and becoming and ask others to help us safeguard against it.

We tend to hate people who are arrogant all the more because we're coming from a place of feeling less than. Intellectually, we know that the person who is conceited is simply overcompensating, but emotionally we hate that person because she thinks she's better than us. We who feel less than resent the hell out of people who trigger our insecurities.

Ok, but insecurities are just reasons why we think we're not good enough. How about we bring them out into the light and take an honest look? Maybe they're not based in truth? Maybe they're just more of a feeling? Maybe they're the result of what some sick person taught us earlier in life? Let's examine them meaningfully, let others weigh in, and then see if we can separate the truth about ourselves from the hurtful lies we've been taught and perpetuate.

There's an excellent chance that our insecurities are based in unfair judgments of self. Also, there's about a 99% chance that whatever we see as lacking in ourselves would never be something we critique others for. Do you think less of you because you need to lose 30 pounds? Do you think less of others for whom that's true? Misfits look for the best in others and the worst in ourselves.

I don't give a damn what anybody looks like, but I love it when I see someone who's 300lbs and carries themselves with grace and dignity. Pretty faces are unremarkable. Attitudes are sexy. Breaking out of societal roles is as simple as breaking the rules.

I am. You are. If you want to become something greater, choose it for yourself and don't allow anyone else the power to dictate what it should be.

- Ok, so let's get down to it: What are your insecurities?
- What proof do you have that these are valid assessments?
- Are they things you can change or are you powerless over them?
- Describe your attitude toward self and make some choices about how it will be moving forward?

Erikson and Artistry

Of all the developmental theories I've studied, only one stands out in my mind: Erik Erikson's Stages of Psychosocial Development. Erikson was the first to suggest that children do not necessarily become stuck in a stage when their needs are not met. He argued that they proceed and advance through other stages but that whatever was not attained in one stage would remain a deficit until corrected.

Erikson was also the first to suggest that development does not end in adolescence or early adulthood, but rather, continues throughout the lifespan. That provision alone is why his theory ought to be the only one we use with adults. Yet, to my knowledge, very little has been done to build on the psychosocial developmental theory. There are likely two very important reasons for this:

If we further develop the idea that development is life-long, that would popularize the idea that ongoing and specific forms of growth are personal responsibilities that can be conceptualized, achieved, and measured. Basic, widely accepted beliefs regarding our potential would be debunked, and the notion that "the die is cast" in childhood would go away. We'd move away from being a culture that whines about "figuring it out" and toward pragmatic approaches to becoming something greater than what we currently are.

Second, and more vitally, if we further explore the simple truth that unmet developmental needs create life-long limitations, we would have to determine how exactly those needs could best be met later in life. That's far more artistry than science. The needs of a child being fulfilled in adulthood requires mutually developed (healer and client) and a lot of creativity. This seems like far more responsibility than we care to take on collectively.

When we consider basic needs like bonding and attachment, we envision approaches that are useful for treating attachment disorders in children and (expected) personality disorders in adults. If we consider more subtle aspects of how unhealthy experiences blur the lines of "met" and "unmet" developmental needs, we approximate the foundational aspects of why a high percentage of our clients struggle to love, be loved, and live fulfilling lives. There are many shades of gray in Erikson's model that seem well worth exploring.

A cursory examination of what he categorized as "psychosocial crisis" highlights states and experiences that are at the core of our client's psyches: trust, shame, guilt, doubt, inferiority, identity, isolation, role confusion, intimacy, stagnation, and despair. None of these are black and white, and none of them have clear boundaries between them where we can say definitively "this is where isolation leaves off, and despair begins."

Everything is gray. Trauma, abuse, neglect, self-doubt and false beliefs throw wrenches in our categorical understandings of growing and becoming. Everything that fosters or inhibits growth exists on a continuum and are uniquely experienced by the individual. If these are reasonable premises, then we see that generalizing has extraordinarily limited usefulness in terms of diagnosis, much less treatment.

If we consider a 60-year-old woman who seeks to overcome feelings of inadequacy and fears of intimacy, are we likely to conceptualize her as having gaps in her childhood development? This would vary by one's theoretical orientation. This is why the best clinicians know to tailor treatment to the needs, language, and life experiences of the individual client. It's also a compelling argument for eclecticism. If any given modality may preclude a finding, then why would we choose to use only one?

Further, how often do we ask our clients what they think might work? This is why I love borrowing from Motivational Interviewing – it treats the client as the expert. I worked with a woman in her mid-sixties years ago who bought herself a doll and a teddy bear. By day she talked to the doll and nurtured it as a symbolic representation of self. She slept with the bear and recalled a treasured memory of a grandmother who made her feel safe and had given her a teddy bear.

The argument against eclecticism is that we cannot effectively research what it is that is working or not working. This assumes that the nature of our work can, in fact, be accurately measured and that approaches that show benefit can be effectively replicated. These concepts are highly applicable within the medical model and largely useless in overcoming anything of a subjective nature.

Our approaches are better envisioned as artistry and spirituality. How does a forty-five-year-old man fulfill a developmental gap from age five? There's no instruction manual for that. Get creative. Your client has the answers. Find them together.

Your answers?
- What's still missing for you?
- How will you get it?
- Whose help can you enlist?
- Try seeing your life as if it were a client's. What would you suggest?

Why is it so hard to answer, "How are you?"

There's a clinical term every new clinician knows but ideally will spend their careers digging deeper into, "affect incongruent with stated mood." Mood is how you tell me you're doing. Affect is how you appear to be doing. I've sat with hundreds of people who told me they were doing well even as their shoulders were attempting to eat their earlobes. The unexamined cannot be accurately conveyed, and yet, the body communicates (with varying degrees of clarity) what the heart has been trained to conceal.

We know that memory, especially when compromised by mental illness, is an obstacle to optimal functioning, self-regulating, learning, and healing. It is also an obstacle to evaluating and reporting something as simple as mood. I've sat with dozens of survivors who told me, "I don't know," or "I don't remember" with the ring of absolute sincerity in their voice. I noticed their eyes darting rapidly from side to side, and I knew that a <u>part of them did know.</u> As Bessel Van Der Kolk so aptly put it, "the body keeps the score."

We know that socialization dramatically influences human interaction, and this is typically observable in most forms of communication. The short version of that dynamic is that what the individual's internalized beliefs and values allow determines what will be expressed. The client's individual and cultural norms dictate what can and cannot be reported. The man who finds fear unacceptable is unlikely to report it. The woman who finds anger intolerable will not often consciously choose to express. Yet his eyes are wide, and her fists are clenched.

If communicating with vulnerability is unacceptable, then a great deal of experience and meaning literally cannot be conveyed. If trust is not present, then responses are both consciously and subconsciously censored. All the same, health care professionals ought never to ask for trust. Further, it is insufficient that we inspire trust through our behavior. At our best, we support and challenge those we serve to develop greater trust in themselves. Those who engage in self-deception (knowingly and otherwise) have an impaired ability to report because they often struggle to put stock in what they sense or feel. Those who come to trust themselves through our help are afforded a more manageable life and are free to place greater stock in their intuition.

Self-deception is most often observable in the form of professed ignorance. There is a certain level of comfort in not knowing. It absolves the individual of the responsibility to act and an escape from what is not acceptable to feel, think, and remember. The practitioner would do well to instruct the client that to stop being overwhelmed; we must allow ourselves to know what we know. If the goal is integration, then we cannot discard pieces of ourselves no matter how unacceptable we may find them to be.

It's difficult to sense when a client is being less than honest with themselves. Sometimes the story contradicts itself, but more often, there is something in the client's affect that subtly demonstrates internal distress. Our job is to be intuitive listener and notice when something doesn't fit or feel right. A good listener is attentive, connects the dots, forms thoughts and ideas based on what's being said. A great listener notes the silences and body language, and in this way hears *what's not being said.*

I've worked with people who when honest would tell me, "I'm all kinds of fucked up, and I don't even know why." They're not lacking insight. They are fighting a battle between the need to remember/make sense of themselves and their lives, and the unending desire to forget. They're stuck in the dissonance between what they know and what they feel. They're unsure how to resolve conflicting needs (both internally and externally) and tend to have poor efficacy in their decision making.

Trauma does not lend itself to language. To speak the unspeakable...to make overt the darkest of secrets is problematic at best. Before a client is likely to explore their traumatic memories, rapport must be strong. Hypervigilance, intrusive thoughts, flashbacks, shame, depression, and anxiety are all obstacles to being in the here and now, actively engaging with others, and developing a trusting connection.

Again, our goal is not to promote connection to us, but rather to self. This is infinitely more difficult than convincing a client to like or trust us. Survivors I've served are often more comfortable getting to know me than themselves. In recent years, nearly all I have served did not struggle to develop confidence in me or try to test me. I attribute this to two things: Most knew of me by reputation but more importantly, all of them have incredible survival skills that provided them a sense of whether I am a safe and honorable person. My goal has been to target that skillset by naming it and describing how I have seen others transform survival skills into living skills. In this way, the client can envision symptoms as having the potential to become strengths. This form of empowerment is ideal in person-centered trauma recovery.

My starting point in most cases was to ask them to notice what their bodies were telling them. The basics of monitoring the body: increased muscle tension, G.I. distress, flushing, increased heart rate, fast and shallow breathing, facial expressions, sweating, eye movement, and hand gestures/movement. All of these are indicators of what the body experiences and knows even when the conscious mind cannot make sense of current circumstances, environments, and internal states.

My clients have the ability to experience and report these directly, but they must also have the willingness and the mindfulness to do so. So too, I am able to observe nearly all of these things, but I must be willing to trust not only what I perceive, I must be willing to challenge the incongruences. Too often these are subjective in nature. As therapists, it's easy to doubt our perceptions. Early on, it was uncomfortable to name what I saw because I knew it was likely to lead to something very stressful, or else I had no idea what it would lead to.

There are countless ways to trip ourselves up.

Noticing reactions to sensory input is vital to understanding those who have known/are experiencing severe distress. Without identifying both the cause and the nature of these responses, our clients will often seem easily dysregulated or as responding to internal stimuli. Startle responses to sudden or loud noises, discomfort with dim or excessive lighting, or pained reactions to certain smells can easily undermine a client's sense of well-being. Helping them to identify triggers and to respond to them more adaptively improves holistic health and affords a greater sense of stability.

I've sat with hundreds more who told me they were "fine" with their eyes never leaving the floor. Some of these responses were designed to stop me from asking further questions.

Some were clearly seeking to tell me what they suspected (life experience and too often experience with health care providers) I wanted to hear. Still others expected I knew that they meant, "F.I.N.E." (Fucked up, Insecure, Neurotic, and Evasive).

You have to really, really, really listen if you wish to understand. "Active listening" skills and strategies are things you can learn in a half-day seminar, but your motives will be evident in how you use them. If your goal is to impress upon the speaker that you understand, you will summarize, reflect, and ensure that your nonverbals covey, "I hear you."

Being a great listener goes deeper, involves subtler things. Sometimes it's obvious, like when your client won't shut up about their mother but never references their father. Other times you will hear your client endlessly blaming themselves and redirecting negative emotions at themselves, never speaking of how others wronged or hurt them.

To be a great listener requires that we be willing to follow our intuition, be reasonably comfortable with ourselves, and continually grow and heal. Intuition is efficient. Consciously analyzing a client's presentation and narratives is clumsy, cumbersome, and does not necessarily lead to revelations or a genuine expression of support. Being comfortable with oneself allows for challenging and confronting without knowing. Practice and internalizing successes allows us greater confidence and faith in our work and ultimately, in ourselves.

Just as we have perspectives and worldviews that impact how we create meaning, make connections and draw inferences, so too we have filters that sort, organize, and shape how we collect information and assign significance. I stumbled upon the concept of filters in working with a musician years ago. I have found great benefit in learning the language of each of my clients and making key concepts analogous to their healing processes.

My gent was a classic example of the gender divide in that he was filtering his wife's communication by seeking to determine what it was she wanted him to do. He filtered out everything that was not familiar and relatable. This caused him to be chronically surprised and frequently disappointing to his wife. In meeting with them, it was obvious that her communication style was very clear – when she wanted him to do something, she would ask very clearly and directly.

When she wanted him to simply listen, she was more or less thinking out loud, and it seemed clear that simply by speaking her thoughts she gained a greater understanding of herself.

That's one of the very best benefits of talk therapy – you get to hear yourself say things and ideally, you attain a deeper understanding of yourself. The role of a healer/helper is to challenge the thinking, notice the themes, reflect the message and above all, to truly seek to understand. That requires identifying our biases, tabling our values and beliefs and being comfortable enough with ourselves to catch the ways in which our ego says, "They shouldn't be/see/think/feel that way."

In the case of the musician, when he explained to me his love for audio equipment, I recognized that the concept naturally lent itself to being flipped so I could explain the disconnect between what his wife said and what he heard. As healers, if we can listen carefully and describe things in language and concepts our clients readily understand, our work is made easier and more effective. But it requires careful listening, a good dose of intuition, and a willingness to sometimes leap before we look.

- Take a long look at your filters. What needs to be removed or shifted?

- How aware are you at noticing your own body when you're working? Healers tend to have terrible problems related to posture because we lean toward pain.
- Be brutally honest – are there paths you choose not to take because you don't know where they lead or because they don't fit neatly into a 50-minute hour?

Reaching Survivors

I love the cutters, burners, bingers and purgers, the anorexic, the phobic, and the folks who are otherwise fucked six ways to Sunday. They're me, and I'm them. We're survivors looking for both reasons and instructions on how to live. Treating us is not science, it's art, and it hinges on forging connections. When we bond, it is according to this rule: "Show me that you dare to bear witness without judgment and, in time, I'll bare my soul to you."

Pursue connection patiently. Adages ring true – we don't care how much you know until we know how much you care. That's only the first step though. Show me that you can handle it – that I don't need to protect you from me. I'll show you the broken pieces of me one at a time. Then maybe you can help me see how they fit together. The early stages of trauma therapy are very much like putting a jigsaw puzzle together in the dark. You have to get a feel for where things fit. It takes a lot of work to even partially see them, and you may never fully understand their contours, never put the whole puzzle together correctly and in full.

Everyone wants to feel whole, and no one wants to explain or tell the stories of the missing pieces. Trauma is everything. Everything is trauma. We need to stop providing treatment categorically and recognize that, for our purposes, there is no meaningful distinction between abuse, neglect, horrible heartache, betrayal, violation, or intolerable loss. It's all the same thing. We must approach it not from our favorite modality, but according to the ways in which intolerable pain and fear impair functioning and rob quality of life.

Improving basic stability and safety are the keys to increasing both functionality and efficacy in treatment. The best way to enhance stability and safety is to consider everything our clients do that undermines them. Denial, rationalization, justification, and minimization are the most common strategies. We tend to be so focused on modifying behaviors (substance use, self-harm, eating disorders) that we miss not only why they started in the first place, but also what enables them to perpetually manifest despite overwhelming costs.

When we focus on behavioral change alone, it's akin to melting the tip of an iceberg – it doesn't stop self-destruction, it just makes it harder to see.
We're addressing not the cause of the disease, but its symptoms. What's at the core? What drives the client to do what they do? There's a lot to sort through, but that's always the heart of our quest.

We must urge those we serve to cease comparing their pain to anyone else's. Their pain is their pain is their pain. There will always be others who have it "worse," but let's be honest and admit that we never look toward those whose pain may be less. Making things relative is a way to falsely minimize their importance. Let things be exactly what they are—no more and no less.

My people love the expression, "It is what it is." Sometimes that's a healthy statement of acceptance and powerlessness. Sometimes it's resignation to disappointment or acknowledging that something simply sucks. But too often it's a cop-out because fuck what it is – what should it be? What could it become?

My success as a clinician is largely a product of assuming nothing. When I hear, "It is what it is," I look for clarification. What exactly is it? Sometimes it's, "I'll never get my parent's approval." Ok, does that mean that nobody else gets input? Does it mean you'll stay stuck believing what they taught you of your worth? When we accept that something can never be, we unlock the doors of what can be.

Misfits seek healthy things from unhealthy people. We wait for folks who never, ever, show up. When we accept the truth (we already know it, but knowing is intellectual and accepting is emotional) we free ourselves to make adaptive choices and be meaningfully supported by healthy people. We must be ever aware of the possibility that our client is settling for less than they can have because they fear the steps necessary to attain or become more. It's not a matter of encouraging them to seek more, or to have what we want for them. **The issue with settling is that no one ever does it honestly.** We have to convince ourselves that this is all we can have, or that to pursue more would be selfish, irresponsible or reckless.

My friend Mick used to say you might not get everything you want but you can always get what you need. Recovery is not about wants. Wants come later, if they come at all.

This is about needs, first, foremost, and always, which is why as counselors we don't talk about "unmet wants." Needs are a useful concept that should be concretely defined individually and holistically. We all have the capacity to continue to grow and become, but whatever need was not met at any particular stage of development will remain a deficit for which the individual compensates and suffers.

My experience is that my clients typically only identify needs toward the bottom of Maslow's Hierarchy. Emotional needs are either unrecognized or dismissed as inconsequential, most often with a false self-deprecating humor. Over twenty years ago, the Eagles had a hit that many of my clients have referenced about their needs: Get Over It.

This message has changed over the years, but the prevailing sentiment remains the same: Forget the past, ignore the feelings, behave as though it never happened. That's what most of us do. We compensate and overcompensate. We conceal our true selves and pretend. We struggle with depression and anxiety, and we use a variety of experiences and substances to cover it all up. This continues until our strategies for not feeling stop working. Therapy is usually a final resort, and the first healthy choice. If we're determined to make lasting and meaningful change, we have to go to the core and consider foundational aspects of our lives. The value of a developmental approach to trauma then is looking at the foundation and noticing the cracks and the gaps and shit that shouldn't be there.

I'd love to have a dollar for every client who has said to me, "It wasn't so bad. They didn't abuse me. They just neglected me." If you work with misfits, you will notice how we use language to manipulate ourselves. "Just" is never about justice. It's about making it sound not so bad. A child who experiences neglect is taught that he does not matter. That's a huge hole in the foundation and however fine a house/life we might build on that, we will always find it falling down.

The most painful holes are the "nevers" as in, "They never:

- told me they were proud of me.
- told me they loved me.
- told me I was good enough.
- showed up at my games.
- came to a recital.
- asked about my day/how I was/what I needed
- hugged me.

The cracks of our foundations are the experiences that made us feel broken. Dissociation allows us to mentally/emotionally check out of a traumatic experience, but there's another fault line added every time we check out. Filling in those gaps is a tall order. One of the greatest joys I have known as a clinician is when my clients ask very basic life questions that they've never felt safe enough to ask.

- How do you have a healthy relationship?
- How can I be a better parent?
- How do you make friends?
- How do you ask for help?
- How do I not take things so personally?

The "shit" my clients refer to is everything at the core that shouldn't be there. It's the betrayal and violation inflicted by sick people. It becomes the ever-replenishing raw material of self-loathing. Drawing out that which was ingrained, exposing the lies that became false beliefs, is one of the greatest challenges to this work.

- I often reference a Shel Silverstein poem Listen to the Mustn'ts - are these the kind of messages you got growing up?
- Leonard Cohen intimated that the truth and the things you most need to make light visible through our cracks. I urge you to consider that very often: our efforts shine the light that allows our clients to see. Too often, we are the sole source of light our clients allow in.
- How brightly then shall you shine?

Mind Fucking

The basics of mind fucking are simple and straightforward: We deceive ourselves through intellectualization, obsession, and distraction. The frequency, duration, and extent of these behaviors are difficult to gauge because we engage in them subconsciously. Exploring some of the most common lies we tell ourselves helps us learn to detect our bullshit.

We most commonly lie to maintain status quo and to avoid both the fear and responsibility of change. It's amazing how lies that make perfect sense in our thoughts sound lame or insane when we speak them aloud. I frequently recommend to my clients that when they're unsure whether something is a good idea to speak it aloud. Better yet, call someone you know will be honest with you and bounce it off them.

Here's a relatively harmless example: "I promised myself I was going to the gym today, but I'm so tired from work I think I'll stay home and relax." In my mind, the emphasis on how hard I've worked is so great that I'll easily overlook the self-pity and avoidance of a commitment that I made to myself. Sharing this with someone who holds me accountable for my goals exposes the lame excuse and reminds me that I'll feel better after I do the thing I don't want to do.

When we dig deep into the lies; we find that we're doing it backwards. We try to become emotionally comfortable with the actions of change before we undertake them. That's mind fucking in a nutshell: backward thinking. Logically we know that the adjustment is only possible after the change. Instead of coping or seeking support from others, we manipulate our own perspectives.

The biggest difficulty with unfucking our minds is that this very way of dealing used to be adaptive, used to, in its twisted way, make a certain kind of sense. For example: Our abusers hurt us. Part of our survival required we learn strategies of self-blame. This afforded us the necessary illusion of control. We reasoned that the abuser was not responsible for their behavior; WE were. This afforded us the necessary illusion of control, which usually manifested in some variation of perfectionism: If we did everything very, very good, then no one would be angry, and everything would be okay.

As I mentioned, seeking the illusion of control makes sense. After all, if we admit to ourselves that our abuser is responsible for his behavior, we then have no control over that. It's his decision alone regarding if and when the abuse continues. Therefore, we are powerless. And if we accept powerlessness in the midst of abuse then we would have been met with despair.

The costs of seeking excessive control are incalculable. The behaviors and mindset don't self-correct when we're free of abusive circumstances. They become ingrained habits founded in a once adaptive, now maladaptive perspective. To change what was ingrained begins with making the processes overt. This is why I'm such a fan of journaling. Things often look worse in black and white, but we can't change them until we see them clearly.

Alternatively, mind fucking is like forcing a stick shift car that's moving forward into reverse. We notice how we feel about something. The emotion(s) triggers thoughts, which generates a solution in the form of a clear course of action. We then have feelings about the solution and begin backpedaling furiously. We will find fault with the logic that generated the solution and double down by telling ourselves we're wrong to feel in a way that generated so much faulty reasoning.

To reason away feelings is inherently unhealthy but unfortunately efficient. It's much easier in the moment to tell ourselves that, "They didn't mean it" than it is to acknowledge someone hurt us. These are lies we're well versed in. We who tend to show great integrity and make no excuses when we screw up will readily excuse away the bad behavior of others. Trace that lesson back to where it started.

Now stop making it okay that people mistreat you. These are the third and fourth dimensions of mind fucking: We excuse their behavior and assign positive intent. **We create internal conflict by avoiding external conflict**. As uncomfortable as it is to allow ourselves to feel hurt or angry, we get in our own way by believing the only other alternative is to address it directly with the person who caused us harm.

This triggers the fear of confrontation. We then easily convince ourselves that, "It's not worth it" (translation: I'm not worth it) and begin backpedaling again.

If we choose to focus on resolving only our internal conflicts without an external mandate, we can attain/regain a healthy perspective and learn to cope before having to involve anyone else in the process.

Having attained clarity, we are then likely to convince ourselves that the time to respond has passed and we must now "let it go" (translation: maintain a resentment, wait for it to happen again, and risk exploding or imploding when it does). Warren Buffet once shared a brilliant piece of advice that had been given to him early in his life by an employer; "You never lose the right to tell someone to go to hell." Buffet explained that this is not simply a caution to hold your tongue when emotions run high. It is also an assertion that, no matter how long since the offense, it is always in your rights to seek to have it redressed.

It doesn't matter that the moment passed. We can confront it at any point and free ourselves of resentments. The deciding factors ought to be the degree to which we're invested in a given relationship and the degree to which the other person can be trusted to respond in a healthy manner.

We may conclude that it's not in our best interest to do so, as when, for example, the resentment is with an unreasonable supervisor. In this case, make it a point not only to vent to a supportive person but to seek affirmation and validation from them as well. Sometimes closure requires creativity. That's one more reason why black and white thinking is our nemesis.

Notice the things you share with those who support you. You may find that instead of seeking release, you're engaging some advanced mind fucking by seeking agreement for the constructs you've created. My friends in AA call it wanting someone to "cosign your insanity."

Things people say that sound innocent but rarely are:
- I would hate to think...(What you already know to be true)
- I don't want to believe that... (Because the lie is more comfortable.)

- It would be very disappointing to find… (You're already disappointed).
- It scares me to consider the possibility that … (You're already scared and seeking a co-conspirator in the lie you're telling yourself.)

We have so many coded ways of asking, "Please tell me what I want to hear." To ensure continued growth and healing requires that we involve folks who won't hesitate to call us out. This is no small task. It must be done overtly and by mutual agreement ("Please call me out when it feels like I'm being less than honest with myself.")

Just as with clients, the best service I can provide is to challenge colleagues and supervisees when I think are lying to themselves. I will say so in no uncertain terms. I approach these potentially explosive exchanges by asking their permission to challenge them and by expressing my fears of being misunderstood.

Always lead with your greatest fear. The pressure of concealing it or avoiding it will likely render you less effective than you care to be. Vulnerability is scary stuff, but it simplifies and removes the majority of pitfalls. Ask for patience, open communication, and express a willingness to be wrong.

This is a great place not to use the word, "but" as in, I care about you, but I need to tell you how full of shit you are.

Better to go with, "I care about you. I want to challenge you, and I fear it will damage our relationship."

Depersonalizing

Another strategy for guarding against self-deception is to make whatever situation or scenario you're facing not about you. When we remove ourselves from the equation, clarity follows. We can reasonably ask, "Would I speak to someone else this way? Would I see it this way if it were someone I love instead of me? Would I dispense the same guidance to another that I am giving myself?"

An example: I spoke with a middle-aged woman today who is considering ending an abusive partnership. We were exploring obstacles to her leaving when she sat back, sighed, and said, "I just hate the idea of having to start all over again." On the surface, this looks like someone feeling disappointed and fearful of the future in a way that most can relate to. It seems almost reasonable.

But I asked her to imagine approaching a survivor of domestic violence in the manner in which she was speaking to herself. To say to someone who's actively being abused, "Sure, that's terrible, but think about how hard it will be to start all over." Framed this way, the absurdity of this sentiment was unmistakable, and my client got it immediately. "That sounds so discouraging. She'd start questioning her decision to leave!" Exactly.

She speaks of "trepidation," "apprehension" and "uneasiness." I ask her to consider that those are euphemisms for the same thing: fear. Quite often, my clients feel like I'm nitpicking their language. They're right, but I'm doing it with purpose. Because what I know from experience is that we cannot change what we refuse to name. Water it down, and you'll never overcome it.

Don't tell me you're apprehensive. Don't tell me you're uneasy. Look me in the eye and tell me you're scared shitless. That's one hell of a start.

These days it seems that no one is scared, yet everyone has anxiety. No one is sad, yet everyone's depressed. We're individuals who ambitiously seek external success and validation while maintaining internal detachment. Un-mind-fucking ourselves is a natural result of combining the Keep It Simple System and rigorous honesty with self.

Any time I'm feeling anxious or unbalanced, I ask myself some simple questions:

- How am I doing?
- What am I doing? (literally)
- What do I need to do instead?

All three of these questions require absolute candor. I can lie to others without screwing my whole life up, but the minute I lie to myself, I undermine my stability and holistic health.

"How am I doing?" is a complete assessment: in this moment, how am I functioning physically, mentally, emotionally, and spiritually?

"What am I doing?" This is a attempt to find my dysfunction. Very often the answer is something like, "I'm worried about a thing I'm powerless over" or "I'm beating myself up over a mistake." But unless we stop and deliberately ask ourselves what's going on inside us, we're blind to these thought processes. They run in the background, stealthy and malignant, hanging over us like a cloud until we finally stop and ferret them out.

"What do I need to do instead?" This final question is usually answered by simply considering who I need to involve in that process. I can cope by myself, but coping isn't living, and what I've learned repeatedly is that simply bouncing it off someone else increases my accountability, reassures me that it's okay to be human, and is exponentially more effective and efficient than doing it myself.

I can almost hear you railing against that idea. Most of us do, which is part of our problem. It's very likely you've already mind-fucked yourself with the word "independence." Let's call that what it is: fear of involving others in your stuff.

Self-reliance does not mean the exclusion of others. It means that you are someone, but not the only one, you can rely on holistically. Our self-limiting behaviors undermine our dependability. Paraphrasing Einstein, the hamster wheel that created the problem will not find the solution.

It's a fine line between changing our mindset and simply finding new and more sophisticated ways to mind fuck ourselves.

Telling the difference between the two can be difficult, especially if you're still tied to the false idea of "independence" and trying to do it all on your own. The simple truth is that we don't (nor should we) trust ourselves to do this. Better to involve others. We're not imposing on them. If anything, we're giving them a break from their own craziness. The world doesn't need more well-meaning martyrs who say stupid shit like, "I got myself into this. I've got to get myself out."

The knots we tie ourselves up in are lessons from the ropes courses of our childhoods. Our struggles are largely the result of faulty thinking based in false beliefs. The idea that we can change all of that from the inside is very simply a lie.

As my friends in recovery say, "You can't think your way into a new way of living. You have to live your way into a new way of thinking."

Please consider:

- Vulnerability is the key to optimal communication.
- Examine your self-talk closely. How vulnerable are you with you?
- What do you believe that isn't true?
- How often and purposefully do you talk to you?

And Here's How You Actually Do That

One of my biggest criticisms of clinicians is that we talk pretty, but we rarely get down to, "And here's the instructions for how do that." Abstract ideas rarely help people. Application of ideas helps, and the application needs to be as concretely and comprehensively explained as the person in front of you requires.

Think of the cliche, "Let it go." Okay, great. Sounds fantastic, but if you can't or won't boil it down to a set of directions, you might as well remove it from your vocabulary. Without directions, "Let it go" is well-meaning but empty advice that your client doesn't need.

So here are the instructions: **To let something go, you have to identify it, withhold judgment of it, accept it (even if only for this moment), experience/feel it, express it, and consciously release it.** Mindfulness is where this starts. Paying attention to ourselves allows us to notice times when what we're feeling seems disproportionate to what we're experiencing in the here and now.

These are good times to practice a bit of introspection. It's as simple as asking, "When else have I felt this way? What's this connected to? Am I having some fucked up form of déjà vu?" Memories surface naturally when we stop repressing them. The things we bury do not want to stay buried. They'll claw their way to the surface, if only we stop shoveling dirt on them.

This also answers the question of why as we get better we seem to feel worse. Of course it feels worse—for a time. All the crap we've spent our lives trying not to feel is suddenly all coming at us at once. It hurts. It's scary. But as they say, the only way out is through. And in the meantime, we must withhold judgment of ourselves.

Withholding judgment means that we don't tell ourselves stupid shit like, "I shouldn't feel that way." It's too easy for us to shame ourselves out of a feeling. We must accept that our emotional experiences are valid even when they're disproportionate or completely irrational. We're then free to express them in any number of forms: journaling, creative expressions, or simply speaking, yelling, or screaming.

Ideally, we choose to share it with folks who care about us and our well-being. To experience pain alone is to suffer. To share it with others is grieving. Suffering is recycling and reexperiencing, a closed loop, a self-perpetuating cycle. The only release is of pressure, not pain. Grieving, on the other hand, allows us to truly let go of pain. This is the key to becoming free.

Letting go is a process and not an event. If we express pain for five minutes, then that's the amount we get to stop carrying. Most often, when folks tell themselves to "let it go" what they're really saying is, "Stop thinking about that and act like it didn't happen." If we accept letting go as a process, we see endless opportunities to become progressively freer, rather than feeling as though we have to keep working over and over on the same damn thing.

The expressions of "Giving it to God" and "Turning it over" mean the same thing but both require letting go. My recovery friends point out that, "If you turn it over and turn it over without letting go, you'll end up inside-out and upside-down." We put ourselves through a shitload of strife because it's what we're accustomed to. We relive, overanalyze, and repeat patterns, and only when we're sick and tired of being sick and tired do we surrender our battles with self to a Higher Power. This explains my favorite Facebook meme: "Everything I let go of has claw marks on it."

Points for pondering:
- What do you have a death grip on that you need to free yourself of?
- Are you like me? Do you find that the only things you struggle to let go of are things you don't want?

- Do a quick introspective scan. What obligations do you feel?
- How can you be more free?

Powerlessness and Control

Often the hardest aspect of letting go is trusting that our HP can and will manage what we cannot. This requires having faith that there is something greater than self, that it cares, and that He/She/It can, in fact, be depended upon to take care of things. The guidance I give my clients is simple: What do you have to lose? Assuming the thing they need to let go of is indeed something they can't change or control, then whether we trust the Universe or not, it doesn't change the fact that we can't do a damned thing about it. Might as well trust—it feels better.

The good news is that the only things we're powerless over are nouns (other people, places, and things). The better news is that accepting powerlessness will increase your efficiency, effectiveness, and reduce your stress. Most of our wasted time and energy is a result of failing to accept that we cannot control a given situation. When we do accept this, that time and energy is freed up for more productive, less painful things.

The desire for control tends to be our number one character defect. Somehow, we need to believe we control everything in order to feel like we're in of control of ourselves. We are perpetually surprised to find the weight of the world on our shoulders, and we rarely consider who put it there. We are especially prone to attempting to control people whom we do not trust to take care of themselves. We do this with good intentions, convinced that their lives would be so much better if they'd only take the advice that we're not using ourselves. Growth occurs when we acknowledge that most of the time, seeking control outwardly is an unhealthy and unnecessary response to fear.

As therapists, there are times when it's adaptive and important for us to take control of where things are headed. The difficulty is that most of us don't have an off switch for that shit. Again, our professions are more lifestyles and ways of being than they are a nine to five role. Our personal and professional are almost always intertwined, and the latter is much more consciously developed than the former.

When overwhelmed, we'll do well to simply separate: What do we have control over and what don't we? In this way, we make life more manageable. Too often we become stuck in what we see as unacceptable outcomes.

Rather than acknowledge our lack of control, we scheme ways to influence and manipulate. The most common of false beliefs is our sense of being responsible for how everything turns out.

Even if you're the CEO, this is a really bad idea. It undermines people you want to cultivate and shows a lack of faith, which is all the more tragic because it's not about them. It's about allowing fear and insecurity to dictate our decisions. Better to encourage a reasonable amount of risk and to teach autonomy. Not only is this a more honest way of being in the world, but it also tends to result in better outcomes—the very thing we're trying so desperately to control in the first place.

Journal time:
- Manageability is a key concept to recovery of any form. What can you do to make your life more manageable and less stressful?
- Is it possible that what you're trying to help those you serve overcome is something you have yet to let go of?
- How important is control to you?
- What do you use to promote self-control?

Self-doubt sucks

Recently, one of my counselors ran into an unusual problem that caused her to question her professional capabilities. She thought she had a strong understanding of who her client was. By all appearances, they were doing excellent work together. Months later, though, she was confronted with evidence that he had withheld some very basic and important aspects of his identity. Namely, he was a survivor of sexual abuse and had worked his whole life to convince himself, "It never happened."

Her maturity as a clinician was evident in that she did not wrestle endlessly with self-doubt. She came to me only seeking insight.

"How did I miss this?" she asked.

She didn't. He concealed it from her. We can examine his motives for doing so, but more importantly, we can acknowledge that she didn't know to look for it. That is something that only comes with extensive experience.

The client came to her because his life was unsatisfying. He gave her a laundry list of reasons and theories about why he lacks fulfillment. His ideas seemed completely plausible. And my counselor did not yet have the experience to notice the gaps in his narrative. She hadn't yet seen enough incomplete stories to recognize his as such.

People hide things. They do so out of shame, fear, and as avoidance of their internal conflicts. **In order for them to be honest with us, they must first be honest with themselves.** Experience shows us what to look for, and confidence allows us to ask the difficult questions, identify the missing pieces, and confront our clients about how they deceive themselves.

Being a new therapist is terrifying and exhausting, like tap dancing across an unmapped minefield in the dark. We replay sessions in our heads and ask, "Should I have said that? Should I have said it that way? Did I understand correctly when my client said x, y, and z?" We analyze and overthink simple questions like, "Why won't they do simple things to get better like improving their nutrition and exercise?" Occam's razor is our best and least used tool early on.

Much later we learn to ask things like: "Is it possible that my client was simply avoiding when he told me he didn't know?" Not knowing is the easiest form of detachment and the most efficient means by which to avoid taking responsibility. I joke with my clients that the two things I'm most like to hear in sessions are, "I don't know" and "I know. I know. I know."

"I don't know" most often means, "I'm conflicted about that," "I'm not ready to talk about that," or "I don't want to acknowledge that (because saying things makes them more real)."

"I know. I know. I know" most often means, "I am not willing to act on and be held accountable for what I know," "I'm endlessly frustrated with myself for not acting on what I know," or "It just hurts too much to accept what I know."

All of the above are my client's responsibilities, not mine. That's why I love simplicity: I'll ask what my client's needs are and (more importantly) what they're willing to do to get them met. Conditions and contingencies compromise both the process and the outcomes. I've learned that in a very real sense, it doesn't matter how much we want or need something. It matters far more what lengths we'll go to in order to achieve and become.

Willingness becomes the map for therapy, and it will always be based on where clients are prepared to go. Experience has taught me what to ask about what hasn't been spoken. There's always a deeper level to be explored. Knowing when to push and when to back off is something we can only know intuitively.

The problem is we too often allow fear to eclipse our intuition. Pressuring ourselves to perform at a very high level is our default response to fear. We treat ourselves in a way that is diametrically opposed to how we treat clients: Wherever they're at is fine, we'll meet them there. Wherever we're at, unless we're at the top of our game or gurus upon a mountain, is not good enough.

The education we receive as counselors reinforces a pre-existing foundation of compensating for other's illnesses. In this way, our training does both us and our clients a huge disservice.

We're left with the bullshit notion that we can be whatever our clients need us to be - detectives, confidants, instructors, spiritual guides, problem solvers. While it's true that we perform all of these roles, and others, we must do so collaboratively and with consent. And consent has to come from both directions. We must not appoint ourselves in response to the illness we perceive, but we also must not fulfill roles out of a misplaced—if widespread—sense of the need to be omnipotent.

Rationally, we believe in client self-determination. Emotionally, we feel that it's our job to find the answers our clients need when in truth we often haven't identified and asked the most important questions. Therapy can often be reduced to exploring a series of very basic questions that your client asks themselves endlessly:

- Why wasn't I good enough for my parents/caregivers?
- Why did I never make them proud?
- Why didn't they love me?

- Why did they hurt me/abuse me/pick me to victimize?
- How do I move on when I'm stuck in the past?
- How do I change my life for the better?

"Why?" is a useless question with only unsatisfying answers. We help our clients to see that none of these things were of their doing or because of who or how they were. Most often, we help them to see that what they've internalized continues to limit them. **That which was ingrained must be drawn out and consciously modified based on a choice to relate to self with both fairness and respect.**

As painful as this process is, it yields simple and powerful truths. We seek to promote fulfillment, and we know this most often occurs in the context of healthier/more satisfying relationships for our clients. The foundation for this will always be in how they relate to themselves, but the starting point is very often how they relate with healers.

And so it is with us—but we miss that. In therapy, all roads lead back to self, unless you're the therapist. This is precisely why every good therapist needs a therapist.
We need someone to bring us back to ourselves and to help us resolve our well-meaning hypocrisy. This is exactly how I view clinical supervision – at its best, it addresses the same needs as therapy.

The easiest way to distract myself from me is to immerse myself in other people's pain and problems. As a new therapist, I got stuck there. I'd manage to feel guilty about having a good day when I knew so many who lived in darkness.

Recovery adage: "You have to get out of yourself to find yourself." One of the best services I can provide a clinician is to help them get out of their own way. We miss the obvious when we can't clear the way for ourselves. The guilt I experienced is a good example. It went unexamined and therefore untreated. Living with chronic, low-level depression did not in any way help me identify why I was feeling bad. I had to grow tired enough of feeling that way in order to examine it and involve others in determining what to do about it.

My therapist taught me "H.O.W." to get better. Honesty, Openness, and Willingness. My training had taught me to require this of my clients but not of myself. I hid professionally just as I did as a child: Pretend everything is okay and maintain an external focus: "I'm fine! Much more importantly, how are _you_?"

There is so much more vulnerability in receiving than giving. Therapists tend to avoid treatment for themselves. On the rare occasions we seek it, we make lousy clients. We're uncomfortable with reciprocity, much less being served. There's no control in being vulnerable, and so we fear doing precisely what we urge our clients to do. That's the height of hypocrisy, and it needs to stop.

Ok, but really, how are you?
- Consider the parallels in your life: Are the dynamics of your family of origin evident in your life today? Do you gravitate toward people like them? If you dig deeper, will you find that you are trying to get your needs met on a purely subconscious level?
- Are you as deserving as your clients of help and support?
- Are you even half as eager to be helped as you are to help?

Getting Your Shit Together

I worked hard for my reputation as an addictions counselor. My tool box holds two items: a steel-toed boot and a bear hug. Most anyone who finds their way to my office has been warned that if they aren't willing to go to any lengths, they should find a counselor they can bullshit. On rare occasions, I work with a young man or woman who explain their choices as someone else's fault. They are rewarded with a stern and paternalistic lecture about the magic that occurs on your eighteenth birthday, when suddenly and without explanation you become responsible for everything about yourself.

This message is neither mean-spirited nor gratuitous. We do our clients no good by bullshitting them, sugar-coating the truth, or telling them what they want to hear. It may feel good in the moment, but later, in your heart of hearts, you'll know it's a disservice. Better by far to communicate the truth loudly and clearly.

After many years, I can still hear my friend Ardis saying to folks early in recovery, "The first two words of recovery are responsibility and accountability. If you don't have those, you have nothing."

Ardis is one of the most effective clinicians I've ever known. She is remarkably intuitive, intelligent, and can spot self-deception a mile away. As with most people I love, there is a tremendous contrast to her. She's elegant – every bit a lady. She's the best parts of a bygone era that young women would do well to embrace (dignity, grace, self-respect) and yet she will chew you up, spit you out, and curse like a sailor while doing so. I model much of my work after her.

Nearly all of the best lessons I've learned about how to be an effective mental health clinician have come through my experiences as an addictions counselor. Most of these were taught to me by people in recovery. If you're not learning from your clients and from those whose credentials are lower on the hierarchy than yours, you're cheating them and yourself. What's truly extraordinary about being a therapist is that people pay me to learn about an endless array of topics.

Bill Nye said, "Everyone in the world knows something you don't." When we do not see or present ourselves as experts, we are free to learn from everyone. Given that our clients are the experts on themselves, who better to learn from, and who better to direct us toward the solutions?

Addiction recovery treatment is geared toward either abstinence or harm reduction. These are pragmatic considerations that are foundational to recovery. Can we claim to have any corresponding foundation in mental health work? We might argue that the diversity of mental health conditions and how they are individually experienced preclude this possibility. Still, encouraging our clients to make foundational and transformative changes is vastly more prominent in addictions and this deficit seems both glaring and unnecessary.

With recovery, we tend to seek commitments to self from our clients. How explicit are we in these respects with mental health clients? Do we simply expect that they will take personal responsibility, or do we give them a pass on account of their struggles? What are our stated expectations and requirements? We need minimum standards that benefit both ourselves and those we serve.

Early in one's career, it is likely not within our control to place such expectations on mental health clients. The prevailing norms and expectations of our employers are holy decree, and likely feature an admonition about making accountability demands of someone who lives with Major Depressive Disorder. As we gain autonomy professionally, we must develop personal standards to ensure that we are a good match and optimally effective. I do this in the first session. I believe my clients deserve to have a clear sense of what they can expect of me, and in turn what I expect of them. I give them every opportunity not to work with me. I explain that I am incredibly direct and candid. I share that I will not hesitate to confront anything that feels like self-deception, deflection, rationalization, justification, or minimization. I name a few hard expectations, the most important of which is that you have to show up. I have a fair cancellation policy, but the point is if you can't be here, that means someone else can. This is an expectation of respect not only for myself but more importantly, for the other people I serve.

It took me a lot to get comfortable with this straightforward approach, but it's been demonstrated over and over that it saves everyone time, wasted effort, and frustration.

In mental health, the problems are often so vaguely defined that the solutions can't help but be nebulous. We can be willing to plod along, but we must also be willing to challenge and dig for the heart of the matter. In my early years, I sat with far too many people wondering for far too long, "Where the hell is all of this going?"

If I'm asking myself that, do I not have a responsibility to ask my client? Sometimes it's good to wander, but more often, meandering through a session means your client is lost, overwhelmed, and doesn't feel comfortable admitting it. This is especially true of men. I have listened to long, meandering streams of consciousness and my responses were based solely on either what the emotive content was or on what I felt they were avoiding.

My favorite response in times like these is, "Fuck, what?" It's not exactly Cognitive Behavioral Therapy, but it tends to jar people out of whatever they were stuck in. That's the paramount distinction: are we muddling, wandering, or spinning? Muddling is good stuff – it's groping around and trying to find a path. Wandering is either cautiously exploring or going down a bunny trail, and this is largely an intuitive call for the clinician to bring purpose and focus to the proceedings.

Spinning is high-speed avoidance, the result of feeling perpetually overwhelmed. It's exhausting, has little or no value, and can often be dangerous. It is what survivors do when they experience a loss of control and when they're striving to avoid what they see as too painful or frightening to address. Spinning usually involves flooding our senses, schedules, and minds with an unmanageable amount of external commitments that rarely prove beneficial to self.

To break patterns, we must establish a client's willingness to be mindful and to be honest with themselves. Check your assumptions and expectations. How are they shaped by a client's method of payment, presenting reasons for therapy, and whether or not they're mandated or coerced into treatment? To this end, I use a variation of Motivational Interviewing that I stole from a stand-up routine by Richard Pryor.

After he entered recovery, Pryor told a lot of stories about his drug use. In one tale, he depicts projection vividly with a friend who is gently confronting his options to continue using drugs or move toward abstinence and recovery. In the narrative, despite his best efforts to derail the conversation, his friend keeps asking, "What do you wanna do?" That's what I ask. Sometimes I mix it with an old Microsoft slogan: "Where do you want to go today?"

Focus your client. Don't idly witness them staying in the same circular thought and behavior patterns. That's a disservice. Tolkien was right that "Not all those who wander are lost" but a hell of a lot of us are, and we're really good at pretending that we know what we're doing and where we're going, even fooling ourselves into believing it. This false assuredness, of course, stands in sharp contrast to the fact that we're in your office.

Most of us need to be knocked off the fence that we're sitting on and encouraged to view our lives as a procession of choices to be made. Fear invites either passivity or impulsivity, neither of which serve us. Do we dare to be bold? Do we have courage? These are the questions that should be on our intake sheets.

This is why I preach simplicity. What are your options? What do you need to keep and what needs to go? The sooner we get down to it, the sooner I can put myself out of a job. I don't have an evidenced-based approach to know when you're understating your issues, complicating matters, or holding back. I have a gut feeling and I use it. With or without proof, I'll say hugely therapeutic things like, "Liar, liar, pants on fire!"

While this is never well received in the moment, it underscores a difference between those who are willing to go to any lengths and those who are content to stay stuck in the comfort of "figuring it all out." Denial is easy. Change is hard. The mind that has no outside challenge will inevitably and unwittingly maintain status quo.

We all want to become something greater than we are, but few of us are willing to pay the tolls that the journey requires. The role of talented healers is to be an experienced traveler of their own and other's paths. We don't have a map, because there is none. We find our way by inferring the terrain through knowing the adventurer. We have walked many paths, but each has its own meaning, transformation, and destination. Our job is to trust what we intuitively sense and provide input about the sustainability and manageability of two journeys – theirs and ours.

In addiction treatment, we know to spot situations and behaviors that indicate the likelihood of relapse. We guard against it and make plans based not only on what our clients show us but also on what we've seen others experience. Any self-limiting or self-destructive behaviors associated with a mental health condition need not be treated with an appreciably different approach than addiction treatment.

There's a very simple bottom line here: there's no such thing as an addict who does not have a mental health condition. Therefore, what works for the dually diagnosed is likely to work for the person who does not have an addiction but who does have a knack for imploding, exploding, being self-destructive, or simply getting in their own way. If you've walked a number of paths out of hell with folks, it's not important to understand how exactly the paths differ. It's important to learn the things that always work and the things that never work and make recommendations accordingly.

"Addiction is addiction is addiction." In dual diagnosis treatment, it's recognized that focusing on the differences implicit in an addict's drug of choice is not helpful. Always focus on what makes us similar and never on what distinguishes us from one another. In the same vein, recovery is recovery is recovery. Drinking water, eating nutritiously, and being accountable are always good ideas. Spending time in your head, not managing your time and being disorganized are always bad ideas.

Build the foundation, explicitly and measurably. Do all the basics and whatever you're left with that represents some special and unique quirks your client embodies can be dealt with after they're well on their way. Stability and safety are what we build new lives upon, yet these are the conversations we're least likely to have.

In addictions treatment, we know that the majority of our clients have experienced abuse, neglect, and specific traumatic events. The best of us modify early treatment to promote a healthy sense of self-control based in basic need fulfillment. This approach is less common in mental health. Do we check for food insecurity or housing needs? Why not? Do we believe the most basic human needs—food, water, and shelter—are any less important in successful mental health treatment than in addiction treatment?

I want to assume nothing, learn everything, and work like hell to claw and climb with my clients. In addiction treatment, we commonly say that an addict must be willing to do "whatever it takes." Can we as professionals say we are doing whatever it takes in our efforts to understand and optimally treat?

- What is your willingness to learn from those who have lesser credentials than you do?
- How many avenues of input do you allow?

- What can you honestly say that you've learned from your clients recently?
- Are you open to learning from other disciplines and building your own, unique perspective and methodology?

The Similarly Afflicted

I often tell people that I never really had a desire to start my own clinic. What I did have was a burning desire to move away from the dysfunction and inauthenticity that is so rampant in social service agencies. I sought to be the guy I wanted to work for but could not find. The upside of working for so many unhealthy organizations was learning what not to do and developing a strong and distinct sense of what I wanted to build.

The absence of effective supervision and peer support inevitably results in institutions becoming breeding grounds for unhealthy relationships. Affairs, enmeshment, shared forms of unhealthy coping (substance use/other self-destructive behaviors) and backstabbing competition are the prevailing norms. Remember, healthy people don't work in healthcare, so the connections we make are based on what comes most naturally to us – perpetually forming traumatic bonds.

People most readily come together against a common foe. It's "us" against "them." Most often in healthcare we're unified against authority: management, ownership, unreasonable systems and the politics of the field. "They" are undoubtedly deterrents to the honorable work we seek to do, but they also provide cover for our own shortcomings. Blaming them precludes taking responsibility for our needs and dysfunction.

Worse, *aligned against* is not the same as *in mutual support of*. We're emotionally immature people, and as such we focus on sticking it to them, rather than building each other up. The best we seem to manage in terms of mutual support is bellyaching and bad decisions over cocktails after work.

We play the same games in the workplace that we did in our families of origin. Loyalty is black and white, but vulnerability is a dubious proposition. That's why affairs are so common in our professions: people who are ill-equipped to share needs and feelings with one another easily fall into bed with each other. Sex is the culmination of opening up to folks we feel understand us, while our partners stay starved for affection at home because they don't "get it."

We who are self-avoidant long to feel understood. Consciously but fearfully, we attempt connection with colleagues. We enjoy that our shared experiences allow us to skip a lot of explanation. Our desire for kindred spirits too often results in connection to the similarly afflicted without the pursuit of transformation.

We sign off on each other's insanity. We will defend and rationalize the unhealthy behavior of our peers because they're doing the same shit we are. There's a fundamental and unhealthy contrast between how we support our clients and our colleagues.

My clinic is, above all, a safe place for survivors and people who otherwise live with mental illness. That applies to staff every bit as much as those we serve. There are countless intangibles that are involved in creating a safe organization: Authenticity and opportunities to take risks are chief among them. My people do amazing things in support of one another. This happens without regard to status or position. My office manager is one of the most effective social workers I've ever met.

Of all the things I'm immeasurably proud of is the fact that we've never had a help wanted ad. The folks who work for me are members of my chosen family. They're people my HP connected me to. My plans continue to suck and the Universe's plans continue to be awesome.

The closest explanation I can offer for why and how I do what I do is this parallel: Being the father I most wanted to be vindicated a lot of my childhood experiences. Being the employer and supervisor, I most wanted to be has done a great deal to heal me from the scars I accumulated in the field.

Points to consider:
- What are you searching for in terms of a work place?

- Are you somebody people see as a leader?
- Are you creating what you most want to have in your life personally and professionally?
- Who was the best boss you've ever had? What aspects of their approach do you emulate?

What About the Elephants?

The expression "the elephant in the room" refers to secrets and dysfunction that are obvious but unacknowledged. The concept does not dictate what should be done with or about the elephants, only that their presence leaves us pretending that problems and tensions do not exist. As a therapist, I'm good at spotting the obvious and confronting it. All that this requires is sufficient comfort with oneself to tolerate conflict.

The most common responses to naming elephants are anger, defensiveness, and denial. It's best, before opening your mouth, to consider the willingness of others to acknowledge that what we avoid undermines our interactions and quality of relating. We would also do well to consider whether we can live with the repercussions of naming what we perceive. Too often in my career, I have been the only person in an organization pointing toward an obvious problem, and when you do that, the organizational response will most often be that *you* are the problem.

For example, many years ago I was a therapist at an outpatient counseling center in a rural area. My employer was very excited to hire a clinical supervisor with an impressive resume. He'd worked in some of the country's best clinics and taught in prestigious schools. He'd practiced in major metropolitan areas and now desired to live in the country. How lucky for us, to find such an accomplished and cosmopolitan manager who was willing to come to the middle of nowhere! He was, of course, eagerly brought on board.

There was only one problem: More often than not, he came to work drunk and stayed that way. The first time I noticed this, I immediately doubted myself. I knew he was an addictions counselor with long-term recovery under his belt. Surely I was mistaken somehow. But no--very quickly it became obvious that I was correct in my initial assessment. The new clinical supervisor was drunk at work every day, a fact so obvious that you had to will yourself to miss it. He was the elephant in our room—everyone knew, no one was talking about it.

I went to my administrative supervisor and shared my concern privately. I think I said something really eloquent like, "You know Bob is an alcoholic who is currently drunk while seeing clients, right?"
My supervisor looked bewildered, though I know this bewilderment had less to do with the alcoholic in question, and more to do with the fact that I was raising questions about his fitness. She visibly steeled herself and asked, "And just how do you know that?"

I explained that he was stumbling, slurring his speech, and reeked of alcohol. My supervisor grew haughty, explaining that there are a number of medical conditions that could account for his demeanor (translation: you don't see what you see). I suggested that there is only one medical condition associated with smelling like booze. And that was it—my supervisor wanted nothing more to do with this conversation. She said that management (read: not me) would be monitoring my concerns, and that appropriate action would be taken if warranted, but that I should make no further statements to anyone about this (don't name the elephants, especially if they're pink).

The following Friday I was invited to go out for drinks with the whole staff, during that field trip my administrative and clinical supervisors got drunk together. The office gossip was that they went on to become a couple. I was advised that my concerns were baseless, and it was suggested that I clearly had an issue with people who drink. So, to recap: a clinical supervisor who showed up to work drunk was not a problem; rather, the person raising concerns about him was an uptight teetotaler who needed to learn to keep his mouth shut.

Ok, message received. No more talking about the elephants. But drunk elephants are particularly hard to ignore, and so a few months later it came out that the "relaxation therapy" my clinical supervisor engaged in with clients was actually him passing out. The loss of clients who preferred that their clinician not snore during sessions forced the agency to address the issue (because ultimately and always, it's money that matters). Officially, he left due to "health concerns." Not inaccurate, but also not the whole truth. And the whole truth was never acknowledged, much less discussed. That's how it goes in clinics where people behave like "family." They follow the rules of an alcoholic family, they value revenue above all else, and they are far more concerned with the liability of the organization than the well-being of their clients or staff.

      Elephants come in many shapes and sizes. Some are best left unacknowledged, especially when you know the organization isn't willing to do anything about them. What's vital then is to connect with others who are willing to confirm, "Yes, Bob. That's an elephant alright." When you stay too long in the company of crazy colleagues, you'll find that your self-doubt gets steroidal in a hurry.

      Today I have the luxuries of being self-employed and of having a waitlist. I recognize that working for an agency necessitates certain trade-offs and even sacrifices. This is all the more reason to find truly excellent peer support and to be a safe and reliable person for your coworkers. I hope you only work for people who value your talents and insist that you practice excellent self-care. My experience is nothing like that, but today I get to be the boss I needed then.

Do some writing:
- Ethical considerations are too often an area of powerlessness. We can report, conduct ourselves professionally, do everything right, and systems will often continue to fail. Please consider and write about how you tend to handle. Righteous anger, powerlessness, and conflict.
- If you work in a less than healthy organization, what safeguards will you use to ensure you're true to self?
- Whom do you know that is comfortable pointing out elephants? How did they get comfortable with it?

Anorexic Lunch Hours and the Terror of Puppets

The same employer who objected to my discussing active alcoholism amongst our staff placed huge importance on having the staff eat lunch together. This was mandatory, and we were often blessed with visits from senior management who wanted to hear how wonderful everything was. (and never mind if you thought there was an aspect of how we conducted ourselves that was less than wonderful).

Lunch was held in a very small conference room that felt a lot like the dinner table of my family of origin: A group of mentally ill, stressed-out people sitting down together, pretending to be happy to and knowing it would only take one misspoken word to send someone running out of the room in tears (watch out for the invisible landmines and be careful not to trigger anyone with discussion of your cases).

I was often asked why I ate so little for lunch. The truth was I couldn't get out of there fast enough. I had little appetite for food, and even less for the show that took place at that table. The highlight of every one of these mid-day meals was watching my least favorite colleague unpack her lunch. Her ritual began with spreading a piece of wax paper onto the table that had been cleansed with an alcohol wipe. Every lunch she counted out exactly seven almonds. Celery and carrot sticks followed, and half of a tuna fish sandwich without mayo ("lemon juice is so much tastier") completed the meal. She needed 15 minutes to achieve perfect symmetry of these items on the wax paper, and throughout the meal, she looked as though she would prefer being beaten with a hammer than to have to endure anyone watching her eat.

After my experience with my active alcoholic supervisor, I knew better than to address my concerns for her with my superiors. I left her a note privately that simply offered to be supportive if she ever wanted to discuss her struggles. She never spoke to me after that. Last I knew, she is still working as a clinician who specializes in eating disorders and addiction recovery.

Ever go to therapy and wonder why you didn't get better? Take a long look at your clinician before proceeding. Better yet, ask for their personal experience with your challenges, not just their professional expertise. If you notice subtle things, like that your eating disorder therapist is five-and-a-half feet tall but weighs less than 100 pounds, it may be time to move on.

My final presentation in the lunchroom of this (now defunct) clinic was to share the progress I'd been making with an adolescent with developmental disabilities who was a survivor of trauma. I embraced a little too much vulnerability that day and shared that I had a favorite puppet that I used regularly in her sessions. I explained that I had named the puppet, developed a voice for him and was getting some great responses from the client.

My coworkers insisted that I bring the puppet in to lunch and use it to demonstrate the rest of my presentation. I agreed without thinking, went and got Presto the magic rabbit, and used his voice to share clinical findings. Within one minute the staff started talking directly to Presto. They asked him personal questions about each other and about the guy that had his hand up Presto's ass.

Presto said funny things like, "Oh my goodness! You're an especially passive aggressive little bitch, aren't you?" This was pretty funny stuff until the fluffy bunny got carried away, spoke a little too much truth and people left crying. Presto got away with saying everything I ever wanted to, and he didn't even get written up.

When kids talk to a puppet, they are engaging in magical thinking, which is beneficial clinically, not to mention endearing. When adults do it, it's a clear-cut sign of arrested development. It's also really fucking creepy. Our emotional immaturity is what limits us the most.

Let's NOT Have Lunch!

One more lunch story. Years later, I was working for a new clinic and was contacted by a disgruntled therapist who had been dismissed on the same day I'd been hired. This gentleman explained that he was not bitter (why would he be after being fired?). He was concerned for my health and wellness, which was all the more dubious considering we'd never met. He wanted to warn me because he thought perhaps I was too naïve to know my new employer was a crook.

He invited me to have lunch with him and discuss his concerns. I knew him to be an experienced clinician, and so I figured it was better to make a new friend than refuse to hear him out. What I didn't tell him was I already knew everything he was going to say. I knew my employer was an unethical person. What I bullshitted myself into believing was that I could run a separate program under his umbrella without getting any dirt on myself.

As the adage goes, "If you lie down with dogs, you will get up with fleas." My new friend wanted to tell me all about the dogs and exactly what kind of fleas they had. We agreed to meet at a local diner run by folks who live with major mental illnesses. Outwardly, I express my love for self-sustaining non-profits because they can be both transformative and cost-effective. Inwardly, and for no good reason, I loved the idea of someone who lives with schizophrenia was cooking my lunch because I'm weird like that.

We arrived, shook hands, and were seated. We discussed how wonderful this new place was and we took a few minutes to discuss how accomplished my colleague was. We pored over the menus together, and he offered recommendations, which made it all the more surprising when all he ordered was a glass of water. I was surprised and asked if he's already eaten?

"Oh, no. You see, I live with bulimia, and I can't bear to have anyone see me eat." Now, I'm sure there is a sensitive way to respond to a colleague saying this to you in a restaurant, but caught flat-footed the best I could come up with was, "You know, we could have met for coffee..."

He watched me eat a quesadilla the way a peeping Tom watches a woman undress. I swear to God he wiped a tiny bit of drool from the corner of his mouth.
His body language was nothing short of sensual. I couldn't figure out if he wanted to have his way with me or my lunch. The former doesn't faze me, but if I knew it was the latter, I'd have been happy to get him a takeout order.

In between his accusations of my new employer and bragging about his own successes, he asked me to describe the flavors and textures of my lunch. One of the secrets to my success is that when things get weird, I never resist, so I described the bland and boring chicken, cheese and flour tortilla like it was the greatest fucking thing anyone had ever eaten. I'm pretty sure he was painfully erect for the rest of our time together.

The craziest people I know are mental health therapists. Some of them hide their insanity well and most of them don't. I always imagine a very young child putting their hands up in front of their eyes and saying, "Ha! You can't see me!"

I have a mixture of compassion and contempt for folks like my quesadilla voyeur colleague. I have empathy for his pain. I want very much for him to overcome his eating disorder. I hate that anyone ever steeled themselves to go get help and were received by a clinician like him. And that's a slippery slope into righteous anger and judgement that serves no purpose. So instead, I seek to help the next healer and my sincere hope is that as you continue to get better you'll do the same.

- What's your assessment of classmates or colleagues to date?
- How honest are you with yourself about your peers?
- Do you find yourself making comparisons between yourself and them?
- Are you convinced those are valid?

Excellent Peer Support Looks Like This

I've had to try out a lot of deeply fucked up individuals to find my kindred spirits. It's a matter of finding folks with compatible idiosyncrasies and goals. Most of us fall into the trap of comparing scars. What peer support's really about is allowing our souls and not our circumstances to decide who we'll share this amazing, difficult, and deeply weird journey with.

On the surface, the journey is our career. The thing that nobody gives fair warning about is that the work is going to change us profoundly. Our professions are intertwined with our identities. The reasons we get into the field will not be the reasons we remain in it. We're not simply mastering a trade. This is a lifestyle – a way of being. What we're searching for is what sustains and fortifies us in our work. Anything less than that and we're unlikely to be satisfied, much less talented healers that people seek out.

Among the most important choices we'll make is who to bare our souls to. I have been blessed with amazing companions at every point of my adventure. They are members of my chosen family. To say they've been with me through the highs and lows would be a gross understatement. We went through our personal and collective hells together, and took turns leading each other out. The most important thing we did was believe in each other.

My first siblings were Kate and Dave. We worked for the same clinic and each of us gradually took the risk of asking each other the equivalent of, "Is it just me or is this place fucking nuts?" We supported one another as young therapists and became friends outside of work. When I left that clinic to start a new program, I brought both of them with me.

Go to your local skate park and find a kid with fashionably tattered clothes, gauged ears, and a massive attitude. Now cover him in tattoos, age him 30 years, and you'll have my brother, Dave. It was hilarious to watch the reactions of every adult who was new to our clinic. They'd see Dave walking into offices, and you could almost hear their inner dialogue. "Should I notify someone that there's a criminal wandering through the building?"

There's never been a more talented clinician with those who want therapy the least. Dave took deeply scarred little boys, teens, and lost men and helped them grow up.
He was able to do this because, in all the very best ways, he never stopped being a kid. Dave knew how to play, and he engaged his clients to the point that they never realized they were telling him their deepest secrets and greatest pain.

Dave used photography as therapy. He saw the connection between the personal perspective and the camera lens. He was never prouder than when showcasing his client's work. His boys brought their mothers in to see what they'd created. Few of them had dads to bring. Dave was their dad by default, and the lessons he bestowed were the most vital to becoming a man.

Respect for women was at the top of his list. Dave would take the angriest of boys and love them to pieces, but he went hard if they opposed their mothers. I heard more than one lecture. "Do you know what your mother does for you? Do you have any idea how hard she works and the sacrifices she makes? You need to show her gratitude and cooperation, or you and I are going to have some serious problems!"

These were hard conversations, but Dave established enough trust with his clients that they knew even through their anger and shame, that they could trust what he was telling them. The oppositional defiant and conduct disordered alike knew that they had an incredible friend and advocate on their side and, all he asked for was that they learn from his example.

Dave taught me that counseling is a relationship that includes the same traits as all the best kinds of relationships: respect, trust, genuineness, vulnerability, and crystal-clear expectations and boundaries. His example showed me that embracing my inner child was vital to understanding and serving the scared little boys and girls inside of all of us.

Now imagine Pipi Longstocking (a literary, Irish, Dora the Explorer). Now imagine that she never stopped treating life as a grand adventure and probably ate a lot of psychedelics along the way. Give her a genius I.Q. and uncanny intuition, and you'll have my sister, Kate.

When we first worked together, Kate and I became regulars at local restaurants. Our favorite was a place we referred to as "Angry Chinese."
Angry Chinese was run by three women who for the longest time seemed chronically pissed the fuck off—hence the name. We hung around long enough that the women eventually learned to like us. One spring afternoon, after learning we were therapists, they demanded to know, "Why people so miserable?"

It turns out Chinese buffets are a haven for the deeply depressed and obese. No wonder the ladies running the place were so unhappy. They spent all day, every day dealing with miserable folks who were using food to cope.

Kate is a magnet for weirdness, and men of all types are attracted to her. She has a theory about this, though:

"If I'm not attracted to them, then they can't be attracted to me." As absurd as that sounds, you have to see Kate in action to appreciate that it's just her way of being.

It was summer, and we were outside a downtown pub, a place where the homeless gather to panhandle. One of the guys was strumming a guitar. As we walked by he yelled out, "Hey, pretty lady! What kind of music do you like?" Kate did her best to ignore him, but he persisted. To both appease and challenge him, she said, "Rhythm and blues."

What followed was extraordinary on at least a half-dozen levels. That guy could play! He was just getting into a groove when a second homeless guy jumped in and started spitting out some rough-and-tumble scat. You know how great blues singers will lyrically reference great cities known for their music? He did that with a twist of severe mental illness: "Baby, take me down to old Calcutta!"

I was already convulsed with laughter, but the show was just getting underway. The guitar player abruptly stopped, turned to the singer, and yelled, "Hey, man, I saw her first!" I couldn't have stopped laughing if my life depended on it, but Kate was considerably less amused. She gave me a look: *You're an asshole, and it's time to go.* The guitar player persisted, "Man, I told you the last time this happened that I'd knock you out if you come between a beautiful woman and me." There was no doubt in my mind that a fight was about to break out. I said something lame like, "Can't we all just get along?" and gave them each five bucks.

Gallows humor and reveling in the absurdity of life were part of how we stayed semi-sane. Kate is cut from the same cloth I am. We're both drawn to the worst prognoses. The more past professionals failed to evoke change, the deeper the levels of trauma, the more compelling cases are to us. The difference between us is that she routinely does things that every expert in mental health would say cannot be done.

Kate taught me to appreciate myself and the impact I have on others. She called me out a thousand times on avoiding and devaluing myself. She marveled at my insanity, held me accountable for being a human doer, and most of all, challenged me to take care of myself. In the end, I may have been her toughest case.

- Who's in your life that you know is more than a little weird?
- Do you lack such people? Do you seek them out?
- Are you weird? Do you have a freak flag? Do you let it fly?

Hire People to Do What You Suck At

I've long joked that I will one day write a book about how not to start a business. I'm fairly confident I have made every mistake possible in developing and maintaining a social service agency. These screw-ups were largely a product of failing to understand my limitations and seek help when I needed it. My new business undertakings are similar to my old ones in only one respect; they're all approached with an utter lack of poise and preparation.

I am not a businessperson. I suck at budgeting, organizing, marketing, and all administrative duties. I can't even create an Excel spreadsheet. I accept this about myself today. Back then, for better and for worse, I never used to let the fact that I had no idea what I was doing stop me from trying it anyway.

I started an agency with two business partners and in short order found myself the sole proprietor of an agency on the verge of bankruptcy. My wife had a perfectly good day job where she could do more or less as she pleased. Running an agency was never something she planned to do. Nevertheless, when it became clear that left to my own devices I would run my own agency into the ground, she stepped in. Without her business savvy—and her willingness to harness it on my behalf—my agency would have failed.

To say that she keeps me grounded doesn't begin to tell the story. Once I was trying to schedule a lunch date with a professional I wanted to hire. My wife knew we weren't ready to expand the business, but rather than fight with me about it, she convinced me, for six months, that the person I was trying to meet with never had time available when we did. When she decided we *were* finally ready to expand, the lunch miraculously happened. She had a good laugh when I commented on how odd it had been that we'd found it so difficult to meet for so long.

My wife taught me how to say, "No" (although I pulled up short of practicing in front of a mirror like she wanted me to). She showed me how to delegate, and to trust but verify that the people you hire do what you tell them to do. She taught me things I thought I already knew, like profound respect for my administrative team.
I always knew that these folks have all the real power, but by being forced to learn what they do and how they do it, my respect grew exponentially.

If I had to organize people like me for a living, I would quickly become a beachcomber, or get a lobotomy. Clinicians are a huge pain in the ass. We tend to have quirks and eccentricities that our clients and mothers find endearing, but the truth is we usually create a lot of strife and unnecessary work for other people. Shit, most of us can't manage to keep a weekly schedule straight.

If you're smart, you'll approach administrative assistants with reverence and make "administrative assistant day" much more than an annual event. Admin are your client's first point of contact, and they put out fires frequently and effectively even though they're not trained to. They're usually the ones to call the cops and ambulances, and they do an awful lot to make you look good in the midst of daily chaos. The true value of a good administrator can never be known, because when they do their job well problems are solved before you even know they existed. If you get through a week without your clinic burning down or being foreclosed on, thank an administrator, because they're the only reason the place is still standing and operational.

Never have I seen a person work as hard as my wife to create a system that largely operates without her. That's humility – build it so that the business doesn't depend on you. People like you and I approach professional undertakings the same way we do personal ones. We like the feeling of being needed. It feels like love. My wife is far healthier than I am. She shows up to write the checks and make sure everything is running smoothly. She takes long lunches and goes home early.

Smart lady, my wife.

She helped me to see that you don't have to kill yourself to be successful and you don't have to be the star of the show. Giving others a chance to shine inspires greater efforts and results. Invest continuously in your people, and you'll be repaid with loyalty that money cannot buy.

There's nothing about being good at what we do that qualifies us to run a business. If you're very lucky, you have someone like my wife to fix your mistakes, point out where you're wrong or otherwise clueless, and leverage her own expertise to the benefit of you and everyone who works for you. But if ever you should have the bright idea of going into business with your spouse or partner, you should have your head examined immediately. It is a testament to the strength of our union that we haven't killed each other a hundred times over.

Homework:
- Have an honest discussion with someone who knows you and your work well. Where do you need to invest and what do you just need to stay the hell away from?
- Make sure you have people in your life who will not hesitate to tell you when you're wrong. The biggest piece of my professional success has come from surrounding myself with powerful women.

- You may believe yourself to be a humble person. Consider that the next time you screw something up.

We Need All the Help We Can Get

In the absence of external accountability, I lie to me. A lot.

The Universe has ensured I always have someone in my field that is reasonably healthy, willing, and able to catch me lying to myself. I have found that being vulnerable with these folks pays off in spades. Even when I am doing well, I find I have far less stress by allowing myself to be challenged and asking for reality checks. This ensures that I wrestle far less with self-doubt and don't overthink things.

Accepting input gracefully takes a lot of practice. Being called out is like being told, "No." We're being confronted about the limits we don't want to accept or the conflict we're trying to avoid (most often with ourselves). It's much easier for us to formulate a compelling argument on the spot than it is to accept the very input we asked for.

To confront requires some degree of security in self and either necessity or genuine caring, which is why so many of us are bad at it. Insecurity leaves us second-guessing, and when we're anxious, we can easily talk ourselves out of doing the right thing to do. My experience has been that calling people out is one of the greatest services I can provide – especially when the person I'm calling out is a professional.

I will usually ask permission because this lowers defensiveness and increases curiosity. I will never argue the point, but I will stay true to myself. As a supervisor, I see it as protecting both my employees and our clients. As a colleague, I see it as simply an act of caring. To further ensure my message is received, I'll speak about my experience being where I think they're at and how I didn't face it until it was too late.

The more we give one another opportunities to correct course and save face at the same time, the more our collective dignity is promoted. None of us likes our limits and nearly all of us want to do more and be more. It helps to be reminded that we are enough. A friend of mine confronted my insatiability with grace by saying, "If you never do another good deed as long as you live; you have already done more than enough."

She was right. There's a picture that hangs in my office. It shows a prominent tattoo that's an answer to questions asked in a poem by Anis Mojgani "Here Am I." Google or Youtube that before you continue.

Here are my answers: I am something special. I am somebody. I matter. I am good enough, and I have nothing to prove to anyone, especially myself. Constantly striving does not make me more. It makes me exhausted. Relaxing makes it possible to do better work, and both nurturing and allowing others to nurture my soul is what makes me most effective as a healer and helper.

Journaling:
- What's your answer to Mojgani?
- How could it be better?
- Take ten minutes right now and write about it. Then get brave and email it to someone who will hold you accountable for it.

On Ethics and Getting Laid

The first time they told me in grad school that I must not have sex with my clients, I couldn't believe this was something that needed to be said. Over the course of my studies, I was warned at least two dozen times further that I must never do this. I finally asked why there should be so much safeguarding against such an obviously egregious act, and I was referred to the state website where the list of people who lost their professional licenses for ethics violations was displayed. My jaw stayed on the floor for a long time after reading that.

Our work is intimate, and the temptation to commit this most basic violation can be strong, especially when our personal needs are not met. But just because I understand how it can happen doesn't mean I excuse it at all. In fact, I view it as a gross abuse of power that is largely indistinguishable from rape. Here's what I find interesting:

Not once in grad school did they tell me that I must never fuck my coworkers, support staff, or supervisors. Affairs among health care professionals are so common that they barely warrant mention, except when they happen (as they frequently do) in fast-forward at conferences and seminars.

The contrast is glaring. We teach ethics as a means of safeguarding clients and the reputation/standing of the professional. We don't address the needs of the person entering the field nor emphasize the importance of getting them met. We assume that the personal safety of the professional is intact and are only concerned if a client is violent or prone to making accusations.

We need to conceptualize safety as the fulfillment of basic needs coupled with a commitment to ongoing growth and continued healing. We got into our fields for personal reasons. We are all here because we are not all here. The only sensible approach is to be as my friends in addiction recovery say, "a work in progress."

We're people who live with mental illness and we often struggle to identify our needs, much less get them met. Most of us were shocked the first time we looked at Maslow's Hierarchy and saw that sex was listed as such a base need. We're trying to save the world. Why would we need to be concerned about how often we get laid?

We crave sex for release and connection. Our work gets in the way of both in a variety of fashions. The most basic aspect of which is that we want to be understood and empathized with. If our partners or potential partners don't work in our field, (and ideally, in our capacity), we don't believe they are capable of getting us. We crave connection with folks who do what we do, overlooking the obvious fact that most of them are as much of a mess as we are.

The work is long and hard. We form bonds based in our shared struggles with vicarious and secondary trauma. The difficulty is that our home and personal lives get what's left over at the end of the day. This, of course, is too often too little. We're exhausted and emotionally spent.

I have found that I need to have both balance and variety in where and how my needs get met. I simply must have people I respect enough that I can relate to about our work (especially tough in rural service delivery and codependent work settings). I need to be vulnerable enough with them that they can challenge me and meaningfully support me. I must also limit my workload enough that I have plenty to give to my partner and others I love outside of my work.

This is no small undertaking. We're not stable people. We're folks who want to believe that covering both extremes approximates balance. We practice "firehouse management." We focus on an area of our lives that we've identified as lacking, only to find that something has dropped off while we were hyper-focused. We rush to the next which begets the next.

Given that lifestyle, affairs are appealing because they're efficient. There's no courtship to the types of trysts we have. There are previously existing familiarity and emotional investment of sorts (colleagues and coworkers), or there's a desire just to be held and valued. We have dinner, we fuck, and we get back to work the next day.

None of this is sustainable or manageable. Even if we're not harming an existing partnership through infidelity and secrecy, we're not making sufficient investment in companionship and the deepest of friendships. Worse, in the absence of ongoing intimacy, we're trusting ourselves to know and care for ourselves. This is a dubious proposition at best. Even on my good days, I don't want the stress of being the only one monitoring my well-being.

Check-in time:
- What's the importance of sex in your life? Any unmet needs there?
- Who and what in your life are you intimate with?
- Are you able to be home when you're home?

All the Shit You're Not Supposed to Say

There's this ongoing phenomenon in our culture in which what's shocking one day becomes accepted and even celebrated the next. There was a time in which Elvis Presley and the Beatles were extremely controversial. Today they're nostalgia, and it's hard to imagine anyone objecting to their music, their haircuts, or their dancing. The same kind of thing happened with tattoos, body piercings, and a wealth of other cultural expressions.

There was a time too when shows like Dr. Phil were controversial and way outside of the box. That time is long past. Mental health conditions, addictions, and even self-harm behaviors have become part of our social vernacular and awareness. We are a society that enjoys exploring other people's pathology and weirdness. We watch television shows about interventions, hoarders, and serial killers.

Our fascination with the pathological is surpassed only by our propensity to inaccurately conceptualize it. At some point in our pop culture history, men stopped having "crazy ex-girlfriends" and started referring to women who don't tolerate their bullshit as, "Bi-polar." Obviously, the number of women living in the U.S. with Bi-polar disorder is far fewer than their ex-boyfriends would have us believe.

So too, the number is far fewer than the Big Pharma ads I'm seeing geared toward women who have "Bi-polar depression." It seems these women are blissfully free of manic symptoms or hypo-mania and are experiencing a form of depression that cannot possibly be explained by menopause, post-partum depression, thyroid problems, or an unsatisfying life. How we conceptualize problems has everything to do with how we create and market solutions.

The application here clinically is that some suggestions I'd offered earlier in my career seem to have moved from scandalous to semi-reasonable and I'm fascinated as to how this happens. In my earliest days of being a therapist, when a parent would ask me whether or not to try their child on stimulant medication for what appeared to be ADHD, I would suggest that they give the child a six-pack of Mountain Dew. All stimulants affect an individual the same way. If caffeine made him calm, there was a good chance Adderall would be helpful.

In the past, that was usually met with dismay and contempt. Nowadays it's received fairly well. What changed? Well, our attitude toward medications has, our awareness of Attention Deficit Disorder has, and even Mountain Dew has become less concerning due to the proliferation of "energy drinks." **Human needs don't change all that much or all that**

quickly. How we conceptualize them, judge them, and respond to them does.

In my office hangs a quote from Freud: "Before you diagnose yourself with depression or low self-esteem, first check to make sure that you're not, in fact, simply surrounded by assholes." That sign has hung for over a decade. Maybe it's a shift in my clientele that folks find it funny whereas they used to find it off-putting. Maybe it's further desensitization in which referring to people as "assholes" has become more accepted. I'm not sure.

What I do know is that all of this underscores an important aspect of the "silo effect" (what happens when you don't interact with colleagues and mainstream society because you're busy doing what you do). You lose track of what's "normal" in the field and within your culture because you do what you do without thinking too much about it, or having your methods or suppositions challenged by ever-shifting paradigms.

This is true even within our agency. We're an unruly group of misfits, and we're so accepting of each other and how each of us works that we forget other people are out there working very differently. To be completely honest, I think the reason we forget this is because we find the work of an awful lot of practitioners to be disappointing.

I sometimes forget that there are homophobic professionals in the world. I forget that a certain percentage of those who work in our fields are racist, sexist, and intolerant of those with different religions or worldviews. I forget that some people care whether you're a Democrat or Republican and who you voted for. I forget that not everyone trusts their intuition and does what it dictates.

I forget because I find it unacceptable and uninteresting and because ultimately the only thing I care about is whatever works to get someone from where they are to where they want to be. ("An ye harm none, do what ye will.")
I don't fret much about ethical concerns. I trust my clients to tell me what's working and what isn't. I trust them to set boundaries and express their needs.

I forget that most professionals don't understand very much about addiction, much less how to treat it. I forget that my confrontational style is atypical because to me it's necessary and it works. I stop thinking about what I routinely do, and I just do it. My silo has some good folks in it. They're well trained and supervised by me. What could possibly go wrong with this plan?

A lot. Thankfully, very little has. I'm smart enough to surround myself with people who think critically. They don't hesitate to tell me when I'm being ridiculous. They seek new approaches and endeavor to develop and refine their own styles. They're free to explore, and sometimes that means grappling with what happens outside the silo.

I get a strong reminder myself when I return to teaching – whether in a classroom or by supervising my newest intern. Then I am forced to reexamine how I do what I do and why. This is amplified by the fact that I have a great distaste for passive learners. I crave being challenged, and I am open to being wrong. As long as I remain humble, I receive endless opportunities to reexamine and continue learning.

Much earlier in my career, I was not a proponent of using Methadone as Opiate Replacement Therapy (ORT). I remained closed minded and arrogant on the topic because I had had a handful of experiences working with people who were incoherent and severely impaired in their functioning because they were overmedicated. My myopic view was formed based on a very small sample size and a very large ego. I changed my view on Methadone after I found myself treating several individuals who explained that they would have died had it not been for a transitional period of using Methadone.

Despite knowing that my Higher Power is constantly trying to teach me, I remain a slow learner. There are times when my HP finds it necessary to grab my attention, and while I am always grateful for this, my gratitude is felt and expressed long after the lesson has concluded.

Quick: what have you learned over the past couple of decades?

Trainings Suck

Today was a reminder of most of the things I hate in social services all in one room. I got invited to a "provider meeting," which is code for, "We desperately need people to volunteer their professional expertise to our grant-funded project that's unlikely to succeed without five times the amount of participation we're asking for."

When I attend these things, I like to pretend I'm a client seeking support. It's not like that's a stretch; I would love to find my next therapist. I look around the room, and I become profoundly aware of my biases and prejudices. I pick up on things like permanent frown lines, anxious gesticulating, furious knitting, and disapproving looks at my waist-length hair and tattoos. I notice the folks who are wearing more than ten thousand dollars' worth of jewelry, rocking designer clothing and handbags, or otherwise looking like they just returned from a cosmetology appointment.

Always in these settings I'm looking for who's genuine. I'm looking for who's fucked up like me. I'm looking to fulfill the connections I crave.

Yesterday I was one of eighteen providers in the room. I connected with one person, and I invited him to grab coffee with me because my gut says he's well worth knowing. I reserved judgment on two others. The remaining fourteen I concluded were people who haven't had a satisfying orgasm in at least a decade. Untreated providers and lots of fake personas. False benevolence and misguided charity. Folks who don't seem to realize they burned out years ago. Or maybe they know and they're just playing out the string until retirement.

When speaking about clients they use terms like "those people," and "this population," and it's all I can do not to scream, "When you talk about 'those people,' you're talking about *me*. The poor and the working class. The sick and addicted, the mentally ill, the lost and broken. They are my roots, the core of who I am. And you are more like them than you can admit to yourself."

Benevolence is a poorly-disguised form of condescension, a way to reinforce the false healer/client hierarchy and convince ourselves we're not as sick in the head as those we care for. Most anyone can pretend they're not mentally ill, and some of us are damned good at it. This necessitates the wearing of masks, and if there's one thing that's guaranteed to scare the shit out of such people, it's meeting folks that they know can see through them.

It doesn't take remarkable intuition to spot misery. It doesn't take a clinician to spot high levels of depression or anxiety. The neurotics believe they hide in the shadows of serving others. In truth, you wouldn't seek to be of service unless you either desperately need it or have been fortunate enough to receive it.

I have found so much more peace amongst the broken than amongst those who seek to serve us. Nowhere have I been more warmly received than in AA and NA meetings. These are my people. I'm just like them; I just didn't happen to drink or drug as much or as long as they did. We're still cut from the same cloth. When I attend professional gatherings, by contrast, I feel profoundly alone. We started out from similar beginnings, but we chose different paths. Mine is in the company of kindred spirits, and theirs is in the company of other fake people.

I'm a special kind of masochist. When I left that meeting, I rushed across town to another. Distasteful as I find many of my peers, I do enjoy when folks come together for causes that are grassroots and real. If I could figure out how to support these undertakings without ever having to sit in an actual meeting, I'd be overjoyed. Meetings just aren't where the magic happens. They're a necessary evil at best because healers and helpers, no matter how talented we are, tend to suck at coordinating our efforts. This reaffirms my great affinity for administrative assistants.

So, I'm in a meeting with a group of folks who have varying levels of need for Atta boys and Atta girls. **The need for**

validation and recognition are healthy. The ways we go about trying to get them met generally are not. I learned this lesson many years ago, while on a local school board. I complained to a friend about a woman who did countless good deeds but refused to do any of them quietly. When I finished venting my friend simply said, "Yeah, but she does all those good things, huh?"

My ego took the shot it deserved. If folks need me to stand and cheer as they do good deeds, well... That doesn't cost me a thing. If you went out and fed children today and you need me to applaud you, I will gladly do so. I simply wish I lived in a world where folks could ask for the affirmations they need.

But I get it. It's terrifying to simply <u>ask</u>, so we disguise our needs and use humor and righteousness to cover up our vulnerability. We allude and hint and do all manner of crazy shit because we believe it's necessary to do so to get our needs met. We get resentful when folks don't crack the code, and, when it's offered, we deflect the very praise we killed ourselves to earn.

Who's cheating who?

I'm on a board with two people who epitomize the kind of "expert" I never want to be. They're haughty, arrogant, and brusque, offering their opinions as though casting pearls to swine. They're what I feared becoming the first hundred times someone referred to me as an "expert."

The first time I met the dysthymic duo was at a grassroots stakeholders meeting. Within moments of meeting me, they asked what my credentials were. I expected they were looking for how I might best support the organization. In truth, they were seeking to know the amount of power I wield within the hierarchy of our field. Amusingly, our credentials were identical. This left me all the more flummoxed when I felt constantly condescended to and patronized.

At first, I blamed my own arrogance, doubting my gut and perception. My wife, the accountant, set me straight. She never ceases to amaze me with her ability to point out my blind spots. I wish that all of my blind spots were things I cannot see. Too often, they're what I'm not willing to see.

I find it tedious when people are attracted to me sexually. I hate it when people are afraid of me, and I find it infuriating when people compete while I'm trying to cooperate. In so many respects, healers and helpers never move past the maturity they achieved around age 15. The codependent duo resents me because I'm way fucking cooler than they are.
We walk through a meeting room of those we serve to get to the boardroom. Me walking in there is like Norm walking into

the bar from Cheers. Them walking through is a series of averted eyes.

The solution to all this insecurity and unnecessary strife is simple: Wanna make the world a better place? Treat every person you meet like they're the coolest person ever. It's the common denominator of things we all want. Yes, of course, we want to be loved and accepted and wanted and all that good stuff, but what we long for is to be one of the cool kids.

Listen to "Cool Kids" by Echosmith. Pull it up on Youtube right now. I'll wait.

It took me 32 years to realize that I'm cool. I had been misled into believing I was a hopelessly dorky kid that nobody liked. I was ill-informed when I saw myself as poor, uneducated trailer trash. I was wrong about the reasons I was terrified as a young father and I was wrong about my worth at all points before therapy.

My therapist knew the truth, and she helped me discover me. To be cool is simply a choice, but it's one you must muster the courage to make. I was trying to earn the status instead of choosing it for myself. It took me a long time to connect that when people condescend to me, that's not about me. That's them overcompensating. That's their insecurity. I take it personally because it's directed at me and because it feels familiar.

Oh, fuck, yeah...it feels familiar. They don't hear me because they don't value me. Ouch. Thanks for your patience here – I'm putting the pieces together in this moment. It doesn't help that they're older, authoritative and generally uptight. In this section, the author arrives at the disturbing realization he has met two more symbolic representations of his parents. Worse, he has taken to referring to himself in the third person.

Okay, so I resent the disapproval I misperceive. People who are jealous and insecure are not going to be happy that I am well liked. Winning these folks over is as simple as building them up and helping them feel good about themselves and their contributions. Me being cooler is an opportunity. To take a genuine interest in their success is to invest in our success as an organization, both of which endear me to others. These are not mutually exclusive nor are they competing needs.

I didn't join the board because I'm stunningly altruistic. I joined because it made me feel good about myself and about how I spend my time. I'm easily bored and cannot afford to be. The more time I spend investing in myself and in others, the less depressed I am. It just took me a long time to make the connection between boredom and depression and between loneliness and anxiety.

Bored and anxious is what my 12-year-old self believed I was. Hurting and scared would have been closer to the truth. That 12-year-old boy has healed quite a bit, but he spent a couple of decades waiting for me to stop running away from him. I still silence him at times because what he experiences in the here and now is just too often disappointing. I call these the "Oh, cool. Oh, fuck" moments. "Oh, cool. There's something else I can let go of. Oh, fuck. There's something else I have to work through."

It's simple. I'm a person who needs to know a lot of people who are fucked up like me. I need a lot of sensory input, especially music. I need a lot of Atta boys and a lot of love. These things connect me and take me outside of myself. I have come light years in how I relate to me, but there is still far to go. Brief periods of alone time are good, but there's a slippery slope between solitude and isolation.

I wonder:

- Are you cool? Do you choose that for yourself?
- How about your inner child? How integrated are they?
- What investments are you making in you?

Breaking Glass and Kicking Ass

I was still fairly new as a therapist when I met her, a beautiful and brilliant child in "kinship care" (the term for when Child Protective Services places children with extended family). She had been forced against her will to have an abortion because the pregnancy was caused by her father. Her first words to me were an explanation of how "making love with my father was a beautiful expression of our love."

Placing her with an inexperienced male clinician was almost assuredly the result of convenience in scheduling. It was certainly not an ideal setup for treatment, and not a case I was prepared to work with successfully. This girl was around the same age as my daughter, and the idea that her father impregnated her made me hate him instantly. It took me a long time to understand that hating him was a barrier to helping her. This was time she could ill-afford to waste waiting for her therapist to wise up.

In the short term, her life was chaos. Victims of incest are among the most stigmatized trauma survivors, and yet largely invisible to mainstream society. She lived in a small town, where persistent whispers and rumors made an already difficult life that much harder. What's more, the girl's DHS worker could barely stand to be in the same room with her. This

Child Protective worker was a squeamish and burned-out individual who meant well but was a prisoner of her own demons. She struggled with one of the most common difficulties in our work: witnessing the suffering of another, we tend to imagine ourselves in their shoes. Then we cringe, forgetting that this reaction is on full display to the person who is actually suffering.

I did what I could to try and help. When the girl's DHS worker asked for recommendations, I urged that the girl be put on birth control immediately. The DHS woman was incredulous. I explained that the grooming and incest the girl had suffered more often than not resulted in promiscuity. She still didn't get it. Finally, I snapped. "Look," I told her, "maybe the last sexual experience you had was okay, but if it was really fucking disgusting, don't you think you'd want to do it again until it felt better?"

My client had birth control pills and condoms the next day.

Other male therapists likely would have worried about being alone in a room with this girl. I cringe when I speak to professionals who are fearful of their liability before an allegation is ever made. The truth is you can't really do all that much to protect yourself. It's you and a troubled child behind closed doors. I am blessed never to have been accused but I

have not spent one minute in fear of this because focusing on my needs is not why I practice therapy.

Survivors of incest often experience attraction to those who serve them. Nearly all I've served showed crystal clear transference: I am the dad they always wanted. That's natural. The overwhelming majority also experienced some degree of sexual attraction. That too is completely understandable. Given their experiences, the lines are blurred.

To the clinician who is seen as both an idealized parent and lover, my heart goes out to you. This is not a small matter, nor is it easy to reconcile. While it is natural to be attracted to a client's vulnerability, it's also natural to be repulsed at the prospect of sex with any person you feel maternalistically/paternalistically toward. Don't fall into the trap of judging your feelings. You probably caution your clients not to do that, and for good reason.

By the same token, don't judge yourself for being sexually attracted to a client. We never talk about this, and we should. To notice someone's aesthetics and to feel desire for them is simply natural. Rather than judge this, reconcile it. Help yourself by acknowledging the attraction and recommitting that you will never act upon it. Take stock of your needs, make sure they're getting met appropriately, and then hyper focus on why they're before you.

Physical attractiveness affords power in our culture. Notice if you're behaving differently with a client who is attractive even when you're not attracted to them. There's a greater chance you'll overlook something that you'd spot in a heartbeat if they were average looking.

No matter your profession, if your client is even alluding to an attraction, I urge you to address it immediately and directly. I have found the easiest way to do this is to discuss my perception, my willingness to be wrong, and my concern for how this might affect the client and the nature of our work. The most determined of survivors usually seek to address this with me directly because they see it is an obstacle to further progress.

On rare occasions, I managed to overlook this dynamic. I'm an old married guy; the furthest thing from my mind is that someone finds me handsome. My administrative assistants will catch it almost immediately. This is one more reason why truly soliciting and valuing the input and observations of *all of your coworkers* is part of our best practices.

In my personal life, I view attraction from others as irrelevant. In my professional life, it's tedious when it comes from colleagues, but with clients it should be addressed as we would any other potential barrier to treatment (directly and with great patience and kindness).

This is yet one more reason to work perpetually on being and staying comfortable with ourselves. In my experience, the two things healers and helpers are most uncomfortable discussing are sexuality and spirituality. This needs to change. They're two of the most basic things in life, right behind the most basic needs of food, water, and shelter.

The girl made huge gains in therapy, even as she found a seemingly endless number of people to have sex with. Helping her to see many of the lies intrinsic to grooming wasn't difficult. Helping her to learn her worth was.

It was nearly two years before we moved from pain and sadness to anger. It was then a very gradual process from anger to rage. She reached a point of accepting that release and outlets were necessary to continued growth and healing. She was the first to say to me, "Sometimes I just want to break something."

Years ago, working with homeless youth, I would often watch them explode impulsively. They'd destroy something precious to them only to regret it within minutes. My thought was, "What if they could have outlets for destructiveness without the regret?"

When my client can move their eyes from the floor to meet mine, I get chills down my spine. Yes! Fuck, yes! Connection. Truth. Perspectives shift, and new possibilities are created. Everything that interferes with this must go: shame, irrational guilt, rage, and the fear of release are at the top of that list.

My client needed an outlet for rage. We brainstormed. She wanted to break shit. She worked in a convenience store that took returnable bottles.
I worked in a brick building. For $1.20 she purchased 24 bottles and brought them to therapy. I asked her to focus on the pain, the aftermath, the violations, and betrayals. She accessed what she carried at her core and launched an empty beer bottle at the wall.

I fucking love the sound of breaking glass.

It's the perfect metaphor: it is forever broken. It becomes an external representation of our internal experience. It's how we saw ourselves for far too long. It cannot be restored, but we can.

She smashed them all. Halfway through, a group of clients who lived in the rehab of the building came out for a smoke break. They were concerned when they heard the glass, but they laughed when they saw me and asked no questions, finished their cigarettes, and went back inside. A few asked in coming days if they could do that too. My sister and fellow therapist Kate and I began collecting glass in all forms.

When the glass is all gone, there are a few moments of panting, an intense feeling of release and relief, and then, inevitably, the pain follows. I coach them to expect this. Gut-wrenching sobs. Wailing. The sounds of long-buried pain leaving the body are horrible. No human being should have to make them. We cry out as children do.

My client went on to become an extraordinary woman. She is powerful and endlessly empathic. The support and love she gives to others is beyond what words can convey. She got to be what she most wanted to be: a mother. She has beautiful children who experience unconditional love and are fiercely protected by a mom who will walk through hell for any good soul and end any mother fucker who might harm them.

Ultimately, if we do the work, we become our own heroes.

Writing time:
- Who's your hero?
- What rage do you hold inside?
- Does the proposition of breaking glass make you uncomfortable? Is it appealing? Perhaps both?

Safety is Everything

I became a huge believer in the utility of Maslow's Hierarchy early in my outpatient days. Well-meaning folks like case managers and medical professionals refer people to therapy even when the client is up to their ass in alligators. The hierarchy is there for a reason: you can't fix stuff at the top until you've done the necessary work on the foundation. I have sat with homeless individuals who believed they should talk about childhood trauma and people in violent relationships who were referred for treatment for anxiety. These folks were chronically overwhelmed, and somebody told them it was a good idea to look at the ashes of their past while their hair was on fire today.

As my friends in recovery say, "First things first." Counseling can be helpful because it's about dealing with how to make today okay, but therapy is about how the past impacts the present. It just doesn't make sense to unpack bygone wounds if we lack stability and safety today. People need to feel safe before they do regressive work.

The most important aspect of helping others feel safe is to be a safe person. There's a lot to that. The obvious aspects of being calm and nonviolent are things we take for granted. The more vital aspects are things a lot of us struggle with: being truly nonjudgmental, putting our biases aside, being empathic and genuine are ideals we seek to fully embody.

Personas create insurmountable obstacles to helping our clients feel safe. It's simple: too many of us encourage and expect our clients to be vulnerable and authentic while we choose not to be. We're so concerned about boundaries and ethics that we hide our affects and respond in a vaguely autistic manner to our client's pain. That's not empathy, and it sure as hell isn't how any human being should act, much less a clinician.

There are sometimes complications in applying Maslow's Hierarchy, and a good therapist recognizes this and rolls with the punches. The best it's ever been explained to me was by a former client who stated, "It's simple: Every time I get sober, I remember. Every time I remember, I get drunk." Focusing on grounding strategies and coping mechanisms that helped her feel in control of herself in the moment were key to supporting ongoing sobriety, and thus stability. Sometimes—not often—the cart has to come before the horse.

Still, she didn't need to process all her trauma before getting sober. She needed to know how she could feel safe in the midst of intrusive thoughts, flashbacks, and panic attacks. We can teach coping mechanisms before we delve into the why of things. Indeed, we have a responsibility to do so.

When people are anxious or overwhelmed they pace, gesticulate, hyperventilate, catastrophize and spew words. Feeling safe starts with physical control and grounding is the most effective way to do that, so I ask them to sit and push their feet down on the ground as hard as they can. I ask them to focus on breathing. I encourage them not to think but just to be.

Grounding is one of the few times I'll be directive. It's just not okay to sit patiently and watch someone act out of fear and know that what they're doing will make them more afraid. It takes a lot of practice and comfort with oneself to authoritatively direct another person effectively.

I'd love to have a dollar for every person I've sat with who was holding back way too much pain. There's a point at which we just can't keep it in check any longer. At this point, if we're out of control, implosion or explosion are the only options. If we have control, we can consciously choose whether we'll express or repress.

I establish with my clients that I will go wherever they want to go, and I simply ask that they allow me to offer suggestions. I'm powerless to take people places they're not willing to go, but I've had plenty of folks who metaphorically tried to cut themselves open in a first session and bleed out on my rug. I suggest strategies for making the process manageable and sustainable. The person who bleeds in the first session is unlikely to return for a second.

We go from one extreme to the other: repression to overly expressive. Your client will likely regret over sharing and is likely to fear judgment. I'm open to anything, but I often find folks try to tell me their whole life story in an intake session. Make it manageable: Building rapport means establishing a foundation of a safe and sustainable alliance.

Too often, clients feel that they have somehow overwhelmed or hurt me.
It never ceases to amaze me that folks filled with self-loathing show strong concern for my well-being as a witness to their pain. Usually, in such a circumstance, I'll end a session with some variation on this: "I'm honored by everything you've shared with me today. Later today or tomorrow, it's very likely that you'll replay parts of today's session in your mind. When you do, I hope you can keep at the forefront of your thoughts that what you're doing is very healthy. This is messy work. We make it up as we go along. I admire your courage and just want you to know I'm amazed by you!" This is a safeguard against any regret and shame a client may experience.

For those I've served with anorexia nervosa, I want to address medical emergencies before I get into feelings and memories. I also want to solicit preconceived ideas about who I am and how I work. When I have served food addicts, for example, they expect me to direct them in really obvious (and therefore likely insulting) things about their calorie intake.

With food addicts, I'll usually start by asking if they know how to savor? The easiest example is how they experience a large bag of potato chips. Typically, 90% of the bag is eaten without conscious enjoyment. I suggest trying to savor every one. Starting points are about establishing goals and willingness, but they should also be seen as job interviews for the clinician. The more real we are, the more likely we are to have an engaged client who pursues goals because they feel accepted by an authentic and helpful professional.

I've learned to address self-destructive people right up front by saying something like, "If ever it sounds like I'm telling you what to do, please interrupt me and tell me so. I know better than to tell an (addict, alcoholic, gambler, etc.) what to do. One of the common threads amongst us is that we hate authority figures and we can easily revert to oppositionally defiant teenagers when we feel threatened or are triggered.

In the same vein, we also hate hypocrisy. Don't ever suggest what you're unwilling to do, and don't judge what you haven't lived. It's okay if you don't get it, but it's not okay if you try to hide that and go foraging around in the dark. My experience has consistently shown that my clients are willing to teach me about what I don't know and can't relate to. It takes humility to ask and again I urge you to consider: People pay us to learn from them.

> Reflection time:
> - What's your capacity to not think and to just be?
> - Noticing things like holding our breath moves us from subconscious choice to conscious regulation. What types of automatic coping mechanisms do you see in yourself?
> - We're all well-meaning hypocrites. The key is to notice the advice you give but don't take. What's that for you?

Too Smart to Get It

The first was Charlie. He presented with a wealth of survivor guilt. He was malnourished, dosing daily on a large amount of Methadone, terribly anxious and hopelessly depressed. Charlie was an artist. He brought some sketches to his first session as a means of introduction. The charcoal on white paper showed a young man in various fetal position poses, hiding in the shadows, obviously anguished.

The smarter folks are, the simpler I keep things. He was obviously underweight, so I started with his nutrition and appetite. He took a very deep breath and asked if I was sure I really wanted to know? I assured him I did and what followed was an externalized thought process he was going through in every decision about food. "I go to the kitchen, and I inspect the fridge and the cupboards. I consider the nutritional and calorie content of all items. I think about how I'm likely to feel after eating each of the possible items, both emotionally and physically and in terms of how it will affect my digestive tract."

I interrupted him with a very therapeutic, "Holy fucking shit!" His face radiated, "I know, right?!" I handed him a copy of the Tao of Pooh and assigned it as reading before our next session. He came to his next appointment and declared it brilliant. He discussed the relief that simplicity offered, and he summed it up by saying, "I can interrupt intellectualization and downward spirals of thought simply by asking myself, "What would the bear do? Then I do that!"

File that success under "They didn't teach me that in therapy school." The "Keep It Simple System" opened doors for this client that cognitive behavioral therapy would never touch. That's the good stuff, and finding it usually demands that I stop thinking about what I think I know and instead simply be in the moment, open to all possibilities and all inspiration. Sit in the darkness and look for the crack of light Leonard Cohen sang about.

Just Stop It

My latest favorite client has a lot in common with Charlie. She's a brilliant young woman with two Ivy League degrees, but her intellect justifies bad decisions with remarkable efficiency. Sherri's trauma history is extensive, and her support system is minimal. She is successfully in long term recovery from bulimia, heroin addiction, alcoholism, and benzodiazepines (in that order). Her story couldn't be clearer – she trades addiction for addiction but with the twist of sustained abstinence before starting in on the next substance.

At intake, she explained wanting behavioral therapy to overcome daily routines of self-injury, her latest fix.

"No. I won't do that," I told her.

You could have scraped her jaw off the floor. Her anger was momentarily evident but quickly repressed. "Is there a better modality for me that you're trained in?" she asked, and in response I drew a fifteen-year timeline of her successive addictions and showed it to her. She agreed it was accurate.

I asked, "What happens if I help you overcome cutting and burning?"

She was flummoxed. "I don't know where you're going with this!"

I drew her a picture of the Titanic ramming an iceberg. "Let's say we melt the tip of this thing off. Does that make it any less dangerous? You've spent half your life finding new and exciting ways to destroy yourself. Overcoming one form just leads to subconsciously choosing another."

She hung her head. "I never thought about it that way," she said.

That's how useful intellect is when it comes to being fucked up. Barring the extremes of psychosis, there's nothing in a person's brain that makes them inherently self-destructive. Conversely, nothing in our intellect is going to remedy what trauma ingrains.

Those of us who stand on the train tracks, knowing the train is going to hit us are broken-hearted children who desperately crave knowing what safety, nurturance, and protection feel like. Smart's got nothing to do with it.

Things to ponder:
- Do you value behavioral interventions? Are you balancing them by exploring what drives the behavior?
- What's the approach you're most comfortable using? Is it also what you're best at?
- Your answers to the above question likely illustrate the limits of your comfort zone. What can you add to your current approach that might be uncomfortable at first?

Single moms kick ass

Over the years, I've been lucky to serve a plethora of great single moms. They entrusted the care of themselves and their children to my clinics. David took the boys, Kate took the girls, and I reeled the moms in as often as I could.

Kate and Dave have the patience and skills to work with kids, and brought a lot of them back from a darkness that most often destroys. I marveled that they could sit with the little ones who had already been to hell and back, but at the time, they didn't have kids of their own. I think that makes it a lot easier. I never knew how to treat children without imagining my own kids going through what they had. Feeling fatherly or grandfatherly rendered me ineffective as a therapist for children. That's why I stopped early on. You have to learn your limits. Some can be pushed or overcome. Others you just need to stay the fuck away from. It's a form of self-destruction to try to push yourself beyond that which you cannot surmount.

So I work with the moms. Which is a great fit. My respect for these women is unending. Never have I known more honorable folks, and nobody works harder than good single mothers. Nobody. The setup, of course, is that they try to be two parents. Good women compensate for the failures of bad men and too often, blame themselves for their shortcomings and hurtful behavior. I've heard every version of, "It's my fault. I chose to be with him" there is.

The truth that there is never a point at which a woman becomes responsible for the choices a man makes. It's clear-cut, redirected anger that these women pointed at themselves a long time ago. As understandable as that is, it fuels the depression and anxiety of an already stressed out, honorable person.

Of all of them, one mom sticks out in my mind. She apologized to me for having to leave a session one afternoon. When I asked why she had to go, she matter-of-factly explained that she needed to get to the library before it closed to get a book on electrical wiring.

Why was this necessary? Because the wiring in her mobile home was fucked and she needed to fix it herself. How's that for frugal self-sufficiency born of necessity?
People who whine to me about single moms and welfare get their feelings hurt. They don't know what the fuck they're talking about, and I don't hesitate to make this clear to them.

This woman worked, raised children by herself, never left a needy soul without assistance, and fixed her own electrical wiring in her spare time. She organized the poor, pooled resources, and convinced her employer to allow her to buy industrial-sized packages of food at cost. The job didn't provide health insurance or paid time off, but she found a way to get benefits out of it anyway.

It took me damned near a year of persistence to get her to talk to me. She just didn't have time. After a while, she came to see spending an hour with me as an investment that made her life more manageable. The honor of being that kind of support is something I have never become desensitized to.

Over time, we worked through a ton of anxiety and low-level depression and came upon some long-held anger. One frigid night in February, she needed a release and asked to go outside for a cigarette. As we smoked, she fumed and cursed. "I just want to kick something!" she said.

There happened to be a flimsy plastic trash bin that had been left out nearby.

"Go ahead," I said, motioning to the bin. "Kick it. As hard as you can."

She was hesitant, so I deliberately set her off. I talked about the stress she was under and the man who caused it. I asked her to access the anger she had for the pain he'd caused her children. I watched her get in touch with something destructive and powerful. She kicked the trash bin so hard it exploded, hundreds of pieces of plastic flying through the air.

It was beautiful and cathartic. The release and relief were palpable for several moments. "That was awesome," was my therapeutic response. Once again, file under "They don't teach you this in grad school." And this was the way she stopped punishing herself for the abuse she'd endured.

Over the years, I've helped people break all manner of things. It allows us to consciously release the very things that we fight with for self-control. Every piece of raw emotional baggage we release and every inner conflict we resolve makes life more manageable. Life is hard enough without carrying the aftermath and false beliefs of abuse and abandonment.

Check-in:
- What are the lines you can't currently cross?
- What are you doing about those?

Whose Permission do You Need?

Lisa's a talented clinician who never attended to her own healing. Everything about her presentation shows me we'll likely muddle for a long time together. She's got her professional hat on for our first session, interviewing me. I love it when people do this – it ensures that we're a good fit and it seems to reassure folks that when they give me multiple opportunities to expose a bias or ism that I don't.

Five minutes into actual "therapy" I know Lisa lives with complex PTSD. The distinction between acute and chronic PTSD is fairly easy to ascertain, it's the levels and subtleties that are intricate and convoluted. Peeling away layers reveals deeper levels and each preceding level affects the development of those that follow. Every client I've served agrees the "layers of the onion" metaphor is apt.

We know to look for timelines in client narratives: What was the first loss? First experience of abuse? What followed? What was internalized? How did this impact perspective and experiences in their adult lives? How did it affect their view of self and relations with others? What we often fail to appreciate is that the layers of trauma are not like fossil records: You don't just get to dig down in a neat chronology from present to past or past to present. It's rarely, if ever, like that.

Everything comes back to self and all roads, sooner or later, bring us back to our earliest memories. This is a very long, dark, and convoluted path. Being a healer means that you know the basic lay of the land and you have a flashlight (more aptly, you try to be the flashlight).

In most cases, the journey is illuminated for a lousy 50 minutes a week at best. Your client goes back to their real life for the other 167 hours a week. This is why homework, active support and healthy pursuits outside of sessions is so important. I tell my clients that if an hour a week with me were sufficient to change their lives, I'd have a waiting list of millions. I expect a lot from my clients, and I remind them often that passive approaches do not work for us.

Lisa is remarkably passive. It was ingrained in her from her earliest days to be so. Like nearly all of us who grow up with sexual abuse, she never established a clear sense of identity. She learned and embodied the quintessential essence of extreme codependency: Just tell me who you want me to be, and I will be that. This started with her father, transitioned to boyfriends, and culminated with a narcissistic husband.

We met because her doctor had the good sense to understand her symptoms as the effects of longstanding and untreated anxiety. As she put it, "I hate my body, so I don't listen to it." Like many beautiful women, Lisa told me that what she most wanted was to be was invisible. Being attractive too often leaves us feeling exposed and vulnerable. It felt unsafe to be desired. It felt familiar to be degraded.

She left her husband when she started seeing the impact of his narcissism on their children. She was willing to endlessly strive for his approval but could not abide him withholding it from their children. Seeing the intergenerational pattern was a catalyst for change, but it was also another layer of shame.

A lifetime of being what others want and need does nothing to prepare you for identifying and acting upon what you want and need. The overwhelming sense of what she sacrificed and what she got in return seemed too much to bear.

She says things that I've heard from a lot of folks:

- "I'd hate to think..."
- "It's just too painful to realize..."
- "I don't want to believe..."
- "It's overwhelming to see..."

This is how easily we stay stuck:

- Trying not to know what we know
- Trying not to feel what we feel
- Trying to believe what we know is not true
- Trying to remain detached from the parts of self that hurt

Lisa reminds me frequently that she's in her forties yet feels like a 13-year old girl. It's not a coincidence that the more fucked up my clients feel, the more likely they are to remind me at least once a session of their chronological age. There's a sense of urgency created by our awareness of aging. We're terrified that we won't get better at a young enough age to enjoy it.

Lisa has spent a lifetime selflessly loving selfish people. This makes for a very poor return on investment. Worse, it requires ongoing self-deception to continue. The inevitable result is a person who has little trust in self. The biggest mindfuck is that our selflessness is selfish. We are trying to fill an emptiness within us by using someone else, usually without that person's knowledge or consent.

Lisa says, "I cannot act. I can only react." Taking initiative in her own life is terrifying. She's not consciously aware of her fear, and has only a vague sense that everything feels impossible to know and do unless it is for her children (after all, they have the things she lacks: identity and value). This underscores the cost of dissociation and other forms of self-avoidance: it makes even the simplest of choices unmanageable. Decisions as minor as what to have for dinner are unanswerable because they require things she was deprived of: the right to opinions, tastes, preferences, and permission to take action simply because she wants something. Like many of us, when faced with even a benign decision, she's seeking the preferences of someone she does not know--herself.

Everyone wants therapy and healing to be a series of gentle epiphanies, ideally delivered by a wise sage through whom the world progressively makes more and more sense. Maybe at worst you shed a few tears.

Obviously, it doesn't work that way. The most important aspect of good therapy is relational. Ideally, how we relate to our clients (accepting, supportive, loving) models how they can relate to themselves.

Lisa had decades-long patterns of avoiding self. Fortunately, she met a clinician who overcame that. If I were still avoidant of me, my effectiveness in helping her get to know her would be limited at best.

Those who possess survival skills are almost always emotionally immature until we've experienced a LOT of growth and healing. Part of our immaturity is that we hate authority figures and actively seek reasons not to follow their direction. If we spot hypocrisy, we feel justified in ignoring or crucifying the authority figure. Had I not done so much work on me, Lisa would have seen my hypocrisy and balked.

In her more candid moments, Lisa admitted, as each of us sooner or later does, that she felt she needed permission to be and to do as she pleased. I've had countless clients seek that from me. Given that my goal is not to help create dependence (I'm always looking to put myself out of a job) I offer permission in only one way:

"From this day forward, you have my permission to do whatever the fuck you want or need to do, whenever and however you care to."

In nearly all cases, my clients will express discomfort with this idea and will seek exceptions to the rule or cases in which they'd be wrong to live by my decree. My response to them is, "I like steak. I do not like tofu." They stare and await something that makes more sense than this.

"I want you to notice that I did not describe why I have these preferences, I simply do. I do not need to explain or justify them. I choose what I choose. You see me as a person who has the right to do so. I see you the same way."

- What's your comfort level with decision making in your personal life?
- How passive are you in intimate relationships and in relating to self?

Chosen Family

I meet with my "mom" once a month. She is a petite woman who looks for all the world like she should spend every waking moment in an outdated kitchen, baking cookies with small children underfoot. She's convinced that I am brilliant, ridiculously gifted, and the greatest thing that ever happened (along with her 500 or so other children). She is a member of my chosen family.

Now, I have never called her mom, and I have never tolerated her relating to me as her son. My secret is that she has no idea I view her as the mother I always wanted.

That's the weird and wonderful thing about counter-transference. I saw a woman who people like me would have given anything to have as a mom, but I also saw a woman who was only comfortable relating to others as a mother-figure. I asked instead to be her "brother" so that her needs could be part of the relationship. Being a parental figure to someone is a one-way street, and therapy is the only non-reciprocal relationship that is healthy.

Mom and I met because her grandson needed help. I treated him weekly and kept trying to involve her in his treatment. She was extremely fearful and submissive, agreeing to anything I proposed—except when I proposed getting some help for herself. Her grandson's mother had died unexpectedly, and her mission was to raise her daughter's children. Attending to her own needs was the furthest thing from her mind.

It took over six months of suggestions and invitations before she acquiesced. I'm not sure if it was my persistence or simply the ever-increasing weight on her shoulders that finally convinced her to accept a referral. I had planned to send her to a friend of mine and was naively surprised when she insisted on seeing me.

I was someone she had become familiar with. She didn't want to go meet a stranger. But even though we knew one another, it took us a long time to get to the heart of the matter. We started in the present: her perfectionism and impossible expectations of self. At a point in life in which most folks are looking toward retirement, she was raising teenagers. The idea that they'd be given anything short of the best was utterly unacceptable to her.

But there were simple truths that she could neither change nor make up for: the children had been abandoned by their father years ago, and their mother had died in a tragic accident.

It took us years to establish daily life as manageable. We processed her abusive first husband and explored how men's alcoholism had been nearly a constant hindrance in her life. We worked through the unfair comparisons she made between herself and others and overcame areas of insecurity.

We came at last to the heart of the matter – her claustrophobia and everything that caused it.

There's a point in therapy in which further sessions are more comfort and support than they are anything that could be construed as clinically necessary. I have been overly patient at times waiting for my clients to realize that this has occurred. Mom reached that point, and she owned it. She then expressed tremendous guilt about her ongoing desire to continue seeing me.

We met bi-weekly for a time to ease the transition. She steeled herself one day and asked me if I'd consider meeting once monthly on a more or less permanent basis. She explained, as so many have, that, "Nobody listens like you do. I cannot imagine ever telling anyone the kind of things I tell you."

I didn't hesitate to take on this commitment. I will carry it on until one of us dies. I have the honor of supporting someone who makes the world a better place, and all she asks for her incredible efforts is that her insurance pay for an hour a month to process it all. If you object to that idea, then I'm not someone you want to know. The more rigid of professionals would view this as unethical, and I couldn't possibly be less concerned about that.

One of my all-time heroes is the woman who ran the public housing development that mom lives in. For decades now, mom has lived in a four-unit complex. In a remarkable series of it's-not-a-coincidences, mom always managed to have three single mothers with incredible potential living right next to her. Every one of those women became her daughters, and their children became her grandchildren.

I have always respected mom as an intelligent and talented woman. Indeed, I have explained to her countless times that she is more of a social worker than I am. The primary difference is that I am paid to support change and heal heartbreak, and she does it because she believes it's a blessing from God to be able to do so.

The fact that mom and I are family is an unspoken understanding in which we are both convinced that the other person got the better end of the deal by far. She was amongst the very first to suggest that I write a book and it's one of very few things she's ever really asked of me. She is one of five women (my wife, my daughter, and three "moms") who have dramatically impacted the course of my life.

I have been blessed to know a lot of truly great people and to have a rich, chosen family. Their support and challenges have kept me sane and have everything to do with my growth. Like mom, I am far more likely to relate to folks entering my life as a son or daughter than to accept them as brothers and sisters. It may be a natural part of getting older and of transference. The Universe reminds me that I am not here to only give (as one does for children). I am here to receive and to be loved. So are you.

Quick questions:
- What's your default setting in relating to folks?
- How are you most likely to respond to a client seeing you as a friend or as chosen family?

Speaking to the Inner Child

It is always my goal to empower and help my clients see how extraordinary they are. Sometimes I relate to them not as they are but as they were. My work is directed by what I intuitively sense. When my gut tells me that I have stopped talking to a sixty-year-old woman and am now talking to a scared, twelve-year-old girl, I adjust accordingly. I used to have to think to do that. Now it just happens automatically. My clients rarely notice the shift, which is a pretty telling statement about where they're at when my voice suddenly has a lilt, and I'm speaking as one does to young children who are scared.

I have served plenty of survivors who identify the fractionated parts of themselves as being different ages. This awareness is most often the result of a lot of treatment and a ton of investments made on their own or in self-help groups to further their healing. One of the most remarkable clients I have served identified parts of her that were 6, 13, and 16. She could effortlessly identify how each part felt, what they believed, and they could even respond to me in turn.

Regressive therapy is an art, and it's deeply spiritual and intuitive. Nobody ever taught me how to work with profound regression like when a forty-five-year-old man becomes a six-year-old boy. I have simply prayed incessantly, "Please show me what to do and what to say." I don't have a direct pipeline to the Universe, but it's been my experience that something more powerful than myself aligns with my intuition and I allow it to guide my actions.

I found that the more I followed my gut, the more the clients who landed in my office were a good match for me. It's not just that the Universe guides my actions, It also puts the right people in my path. Sometimes only to give, sometimes only to receive, and most often, to do both.

Perhaps there is a way to do this for clients without coming to love them. If there is, I don't want to know it. Those I have served most effectively are people who are very much like me. Our experiences may be very different. By any prevailing social standard, we are very different people. But in the ways that matter most, these folks are kindred spirits.

I have been blessed to believe in people who did not believe in themselves. Teaching them about them taught me a lot about me. THEY taught me a lot about me.

You Fucking Matter

Joan is very young when she's in my office. She feels safe enough to fully be herself. She knows I see what she hides from both the world and herself. We play a game together - I point toward her scars, and she jokes about them.

She finds it unnerving when I don't laugh at her jokes. I smile sadly and tell her what I see: You're very funny, but I feel the truth in your words. You mock your own pain. I understand that you do that to cope, but I also know you'd find it cruel to do that to someone else. You see it as 'It's just me." In your estimation, you don't matter.

But you do matter...a lot...to more folks than I can count. You treat yourself like your mother did. You've devoted your life to being the opposite of her, but you honor her in how you relate to yourself.

There's no freedom in being the opposite of our parents. We're not free to be ourselves because the most crucial part of our way of being is, "Don't be like them." The only way to be unlike their extreme is to go to the other. They were selfish, so we are selfless.

Selfless people don't live in ways that are sustainable or manageable. As we process Joan's quest not to be her mother; she mentions that she calls her mom daily. Ouch. We reach out for what was never there in hopes that it will suddenly, magically appear. Of course, there's no rational basis for this. There's simply an inner child who has waited decades to get their needs met.

The cost of this false hope is perpetual disappointment and rejection of self. Too many of us want to believe, "This time will be different." Inevitably, it isn't, and then instead of being angry with them, we get mad at ourselves for seeking and expecting more than they ever give.

We're people who invest readily in others, but we tend to stick with sick and selfish people who have no willingness or desire to change. There's no age at which we stop needing moms and dads. Too many of us get stuck in the injustice. We don't act in our own best interest because we were taught to deny our needs, wants, and feelings.

There's this terrible binary in which we feel that we must either stay the course and hold out for them or give up on them entirely. I encourage folks to consider that there's a third way. We can simply stop waiting and receive from those who want to give. If ever our family of origin does change, then we can reassess and adjust, but holding out for justice too often results in continued disappointment and, worse, a lonely life.

Tough stuff:
- Are there folks you're holding out for?
- What are you still waiting for?

- How else could you get it?

Filling the Emptiness

For the most part, the adage "Addiction is addiction is addiction" is valid. The only notable exception is food addiction. It's the only substance that a person can become addicted to without the choice of abstinence. This distinction, coupled with my understanding of how those in active addiction tend to behave, directs my approach to treatment in a way that highlights the missing piece in most forms of dual diagnosis treatment: how to fill the emptiness.

I can very accurately predict some aspects of what a client expects me to say and do based on their presenting need. A food addict seeking treatment expects me to tell them to eat less and eat more nutritiously. I'm not going to do any of that. If you somehow became an adult without knowing those things, you need a higher level of service than I can provide.

What I do instead is teach people to enhance their ability to experience the present moment. Again, the big bag of chips is the easiest starting point (bet you notice this the next time you eat chips). Every food addict knows this experience well. We sit down on the couch with the lie that we're not going to eat the whole bag. The problem is that we notice the first bite, the last 10% of the bag, and almost nothing in between. So to feel anything at all, we HAVE to finish the bag—otherwise we don't get to the 10% we actually notice. We're filling an emptiness. We can see the same dynamic in an alcoholic drinking beers. We notice the first sip and the feeling after the sixth beer and everything in between is simply a process of gradually numbing out.

If my goal is to enjoy each chip, that requires that I be mindful. Being present in the moment means I am connected to my body, which results in awareness of satiation. Food addicts don't generally notice that physiological state. We notice when it hurts, and everything preceding that is numbness.

The real problem is that because we live at the extremes, we're only truly engaged when something makes us feel really, really good (excitement, happiness, adrenaline) or when we're in a lot of pain (fear, shame, regret). The rest of the time we're numb, and while we're numb, pressure is building, bad ideas are formulating, and resentments are festering. Every addiction results in increasing periods of numbness. Eventually, we don't use to feel good but to avoid feeling bad— and that's when it's really got you by the balls.

Numbness becomes the preferred alternative to emptiness. We're blocking awareness of what Shel Silverstein wrote about in, "The Missing Piece." We're a sound byte culture with a love of sweet-sounding lies. We want to believe there's a formula of x, y, and z that will make us feel complete. The perfect partner, job, car, and home or some other fucking stupid thing that doesn't stand a chance of making us any happier, more serene, or more at ease.

The choice to abstain (or use food responsibly) is not the solution. Recovery is the solution. Recovery means transformation and building a better life. This requires identifying what the missing pieces are.

The missing pieces are almost always a developmental need(s) that were not met. They're eighty percent what we never internalized that we needed to and twenty percent what we did internalize that no child should have to. They're usually the results of trauma, abuse, and neglect.

Jim is a 45-year-old poly substance and food addict who intrigued me. After twenty years of treatment with some pretty impressive healers, he had shown no measurable improvement in his depression, anxiety, or use of substances. Jim was the first client I'd knowingly served who was decidedly better read and more appraised of current research on trauma than I was. He went to great lengths to impress upon me that he was knowledgeable and had strong insight into his mental health.

He presented it through Erikson's Life Stage Model and directly asked me, "How am I, as a 45-year-old man, to meet the developmental needs of a five-year-old boy?" He described a childhood in which abuse was a daily experience and fear was his baseline emotion. Decades later, his fear remained largely unchanged.

I asked him to stretch his imagination and consider what he would say and do if I sat a five-year-old boy with his experiences and feelings next to him.

He responded angrily. "I would do nothing for fear of making it worse for him!"

I suggested that what he'd be more likely to do was something honest like admitting, "I don't know what's happening, but I'm going to take care of this. You're okay, and I'll make sure you get what you need."

Jim considered that he would indeed be likely to say such things. In doing so, he'd be giving the child both a healthy perspective and reassurance that he was safe. I suggested that this approach was exactly what was missing in how he relates to himself. This is more than a small leap to take. Most folks aren't aware of their self-talk, and they don't conceptualize how they relate to themselves as constituting a relationship.

Jim was his own worst enemy. He was highly avoidant of self, and this left him largely at a loss for identifying what his needs were, much less determining how to meet them. Worse, he was blinded internally by virtue of relying on his astounding intellect. When overwhelmed, Jim would confront his anxiety with rationality and reason that there was nothing in the present to be fearful of. This provided an informed perspective but no relief from his anxiety.

I asked him to consider that a child's fear of the dark is inherently irrational, but to explain to the child that there is nothing present in the dark that is not there in the light is not sufficient to appease the child's fears. The child needs to be nurtured, held, comforted, heard, and reassured with great patience and love.

Jim hid his pain externally through his use of humor. Like most obese people I've known, humor was a way to earn acceptance and cover up emotional vulnerability. He referenced the Eagles song, "Get Over It." Mocking his pain, he sang the song start to finish.

I don't laugh at moments like this. I asked him to consider that mocking his pain was a form of rejecting parts of himself. "It's like making fun of a child for being afraid," I told him.

His face went white, and he stammered, "That's what my family would do to me when I was scared or sad."

Bingo. That's internalization, which in turn became conditioned behavior. We treat ourselves as they did. These are very hard habits to break because they are subconsciously driven. It's what you say to yourself immediately after making a mistake.

Some of us get to say, "Whoops!" and some of us growl, "Nice job, stupid!" Children are unwitting sponges. How you speak to them becomes their inner voice.

Jim's problem was a common one. The unmet need remained an abstract problem seeking a concrete solution. Talking to his inner child was something he just couldn't imagine himself doing, and journaling was something he was not at all open to.

I suggested instead that he volunteer with the Big Brothers/Big Sisters program, ideally with a boy whose chronological age was close to his own emotional range. This can work amazingly well. There is something about being in the company of a young child that brings out the best in a person. It took a long time, but I saw a softening in Jim. The man who avoided himself became focused on meeting the needs of a child. The distractions and addictions became fewer and less intense. He felt a newfound sense of purpose and even his humor moved from being self-deprecating to silliness and enjoying the absurdities of life.

Parenting, volunteering, mentoring, coaching, all of these activities give us the opportunity to give that which was denied us. I believe that if we're honest with ourselves, we find that this is connected to all the reasons we went into our chosen professions.

We seek to inspire and to teach. Too often we have not experienced or come to acceptance of the very things we're trying to facilitate and impart. This leaves a healer feeling fraudulent and unsure about the degree to which we are effective in our work.

The good news is that all of us are to some degree hypocritical. All of us dispense advice that we don't take. I suggest to people that they not smoke despite being a heavy smoker myself. I urge others not to beat themselves up or shame themselves. I would sooner see my defects as a work in progress and my hypocrisy as motivation to get better. Shame inhibits me and inspiration motivates me. I get to choose which to work from.

My inner child will always yearn for a dad. To the greatest extent that I was able, I fathered my children as I wish I had been. This showed me how to parent myself. My challenge to healers is may we relate to ourselves at least as well as we do our clients.

We seek the best in them. We invest in them. We are accepting, encouraging, validating and affirming. If we know how to be this to others, then we know how to be this to ourselves.

Check-in:
- What's the connection like between your adult and child selves?

- What does your inner child most need from you?

Bad Ass Bitch

She's a gifted case manager. The same skill set she once used to get drugs is now leveraged in helping downtrodden women rebuild their lives. It's one of the greatest transformations a person in addiction recovery can make. Manipulation is the primary tool of every active addict. Learn to use those skills for good, and you'll become a force to be reckoned with.

There's just one fatal flaw of course. They'll save everyone but themselves. They'll get clean, do all the right things, but leave the trauma untouched. I confront my case manager's hypocrisy: You don't take the advice you give, and you're careening wildly toward burn out.

I'm going for the hardest sell of all – convincing her that she needs a solid support system of women like herself. "I don't like women," she spits. I remind her that recovery is not based in likes or wants but rather in needs. Predictably, she expects all women to behave to varying degrees as her mother – a woman who pretended the abuse of her daughter wasn't happening.

I remind her that her life mission seems to be being the opposite of her mother. She readily agrees. I then ask if she believes she's the only woman she knows with a life-guiding principle like that? She's abashed. She knows there are others, but the possibility of being vulnerable with them is beyond comprehension.

She sees vulnerability as what a child is when she's raped. There it is – the simple, powerful association that has to be overcome. I ask if she's vulnerable with her children. Of course she is. I ask if she's vulnerable with her husband. She studies my floor.

We talk about her man. He's good. He's trustworthy. She knows she can open up to him, but she won't allow it. She talks about staying busy and being too busy taking care of others to take care of herself.

"No chance you'll come to resent them for that, huh?" I ask.

She falls back on a phrase I've heard far too often, "As long as I'm the only one who gets hurt, it's ok." That is such bullshit. It's justification for what she knows to be unhealthy behavior. If you really believe something, you don't have to justify it. You just assert it.

More importantly, "Where did you learn that it's ok for you to be hurt? Wasn't that a lesson you learned from people who hurt you?"

"I was raped. My step-father took my virginity when I was seven. Ever since then I've just taken care of everyone and not worried about myself." She speaks those words with less emotion that I'd have reading a grocery list.

She tries to change the subject, and I'm not having it. "You just told me you were raped as a child like it was no big deal." It sounds different when someone else says it, especially the first time. She cries silently. After a few moments, I ask her to consider that she's still paying for the pain inflicted many years ago.

I watch her stuff it back down. Her shoulders tense, she holds her breath. Her face regains composure. She wipes away the tears, willing them out of existence.

I play my trump card. "What would you say to a woman in your shoes?"

She glares at me, but she knows I won't let up. "I'd tell her to get her ass to a meeting and get a sponsor and spill her guts, but I don't have time for that!"

Make the time. If you had to make time because your kids or your husband or your clients need something, do you object or do you just find a way to make it happen? "I make it happen." Ok, look, I get it. You're ten feet tall and bullet proof, but you're still heading toward a wall at 100 mph. Take it from somebody who's hit that wall more than a few times. You're not much use to anybody when you crash and burn.

There are no words to convey the respect I have for women like her. She's my people – determined, tenacious, and courageous. She will go above and beyond every time. But she won't cross the street for her own sake. You can do that until you can't.

Challenging the ten feet tall and bulletproof take a lot of security in yourself. More importantly, you have to not be a hypocrite to do it well.

Check-in:
- What's your comfort level with confrontation and conflict?
- How can that improve further?

Let's Talk About Sex (& Awkwardness)

Sex therapy is a respected and important specialty that nonetheless remains somewhat on the periphery of our field. As a result, mainstream therapists are often confronted with sexual dysfunction or (more commonly) complaints about really bad sex lives from our clients. One of the acid tests I use with clinicians is, if you're uncomfortable talking about sex, you're probably not a very effective therapist in general. What's more, I'd also have some predictions about the quality of your sex life.

Anxiety is the biggest barrier to good sex for two main reasons: It makes it hard to relax physically, and to be present emotionally. It also leaves one uncomfortable communicating needs, wants, and feelings. One of the best ways for us to be of service in working with couples is to initiate awkward conversations that result in greater understanding.

Facilitation is largely a matter of doing the thing your client is afraid to do. Initiate the conversation, embrace the awkwardness, and your clients will typically follow your lead. It becomes a "Well, I guess this is happening" moment, and new possibilities are created.

Most couples are so imprisoned by their fears of hurting each other's feelings that they miss out on opportunities to give each other greater fulfillment. Worse, they're usually blinded by mythology and very basic misunderstandings about each other. This is most problematic with heterosexual couples.

Straight women inexplicably expect that men must have at least a very basic understanding of their bodies. I confront this fallacy by referencing the day in 5th-grade health or science class when they separated boys and girls. On that day, the average girl of my generation learned a lot about her body and how it functions. The average boy got some very dubious input about "not pissing in the wind" from a gym teacher, then played dodgeball for the next two hours while the girls got an education.

The average American man believes that women use sex primarily as a form of control and that there's nothing they can do after the newness of a relationship wears off to entice her. He is likely to believe that her libido is naturally much, much lower than his. He will also whine extensively about how difficult it is to either understand or please her.

This underscores the main reason I prefer working with women. There's so much I don't have to explain to them, and I have to explain damn near everything to the average man. Women are not at all difficult to understand; they are simply vastly more aware of things that boys and men are socialized to filter out (most notably, the emotional and relational experiences of others). While as therapists we may take observations like that for granted, it's important to remember that very often, our clients have never considered what we take for granted.

The average man won't understand that for most women, how they feel about their body on any given day will play a large role in whether they're interested in sex. For most men, beer bellies and balding heads don't diminish our desire for sex at all. The tragedy here is that men will often perceive lack of desire on her part as a rejection of him, instead of making the connection that she may be rejecting herself—and, importantly, that he can contribute positively or negatively to this dynamic.

The number one complaint I hear from men is, "She never initiates sex!" The straight women I've served typically have a giant misunderstanding as to what constitutes initiation. I will take the lead on this one and ask her, "You think of initiation as a very forward and seductive thing to do, yes?" She will almost invariably agree. I will then role play, explain I'm playing her part, turn to him and ask, "Hey, do you wanna?"

He will then light up excitedly and explain that he'd LOVE it if she would do this. Her face will show a mix of shock and disbelief. She can't imagine that's all it would take, but it is. I've never served a couple who couldn't reconcile this one. It's an important need that's easily fulfilled, but first you have to remove the fear of asking for what we want, as well as misconceptions of how sex should be approached according to the average beauty magazine, not to mention pornography.

Ellen DeGeneres once did a stand-up comedy routine in which she marveled that some folks video record themselves having sex.
She points out that she can find only one plausible reason to do this: In much the same way that a football coach records games to demonstrate how performance can be improved upon.

As with all good comedy, there's a lot of truth embedded in the jokes. For less fraught and more satisfying sex lives, our clients need to get specific and explicit. Men typically respond well to instruction in the bedroom, but women often have difficulty articulating what they want and need. If she can't bring herself to say it, I'll suggest that she show him. I'm endlessly amused that we can be vulnerable enough to be naked and engaging in sexual acts, but we can't simply talk about them. This fact highlights how many different types of vulnerability there are, and that folks are often comfortable with some but not others.

Sex is a vast subject, but most of us approach it with very limited, categorical thinking. It's also one of the areas of human behavior where we see prominently the impact of mental illness and false beliefs. We know of course that people who are promiscuous are often seeking approval in unhealthy ways, and often our clients are aware of this, too. But they seek to dispel this self-knowledge with self-deprecating humor, referring to their mommy or daddy issues.

It's such a cheap term for a vitally important and foundational issue. Most often what people need explained is why a romantic/sexual partner cannot meet the needs properly fulfilled by a parent. Many have never thought this one through. As obvious as it is, there's no end to the number of clients who will need it broken down for them.

I came to see an Oedipus Complex as something that exists on a very wide spectrum. In a limited sense, most men very much want to be mothered. This is most evident when we're sick. We obviously have a far lower tolerance for discomfort and pain than women, and desperately want to be comforted by women when we are ill.

Extrapolating from this point, the degree to which we want to be mothered is directly proportional to our emotional maturity. For men who grew up being enmeshed or abandoned by their mothers, we look to girlfriends and wives to fulfill us. Here again, we tend not to communicate these desires. We assume that women simply know what we want, no matter how fucked up what we want may be.

For heterosexual women, the mythology goes that the right romantic partner is the key to fulfillment, particularly in light of an unhealthy childhood. I live in a world in which it is fairly normative for girls and young women to refer to their boyfriends as "Daddy." While this term is not exclusive to fatherhood, it suggests that he has far more power and that she requires his protection, his dominance, or at the very least, his penis.

The most difficult work regarding sex is with those who continue to live with frequent dissociation. For most of these folks, sex is experienced at best as a chore. It's a process of fulfilling expectations (perceived or imagined) and something that triggers memories of abuse. Sex is not likely to be a safe pursuit for these people early in treatment.

To an awful lot of survivors, I've suggested that they take a break from seeking a partner and have found that not having sex is a huge boon to trauma recovery. This is such an obvious, common sense notion, but I've rarely heard it spoken. The older we get, the more we despair that we'll never overcome past trauma and the more we fear that we'll die alone. For many of us, this simply results in going from one unhealthy relationship to another and jumping into bed because we feel pressured to or because we don't know what else to do.

One of my favorite homework assignments over the years with women who live with anxiety has been to suggest that they buy a vibrator. I have served hundreds who were ashamed of their bodies, well beyond the basics of distorted body imagery. Their attitudes toward sex are diverse, but their view of masturbation tends not to be. Masturbation can be a great tool for reclaiming and a healthy means by which to gain comfort with one's body and sexuality after basic safety is attained.

Self-exploration:
- What's your comfort level with discussing sex and other sensitive subjects?
- What do you find uncomfortable to process?
- How comfortable are you with your own body?

Defenses, Damsels, Dragons, and Damn...

The most common self-limiting behavior is black and white thinking. We are people who embrace dichotomies because they perpetuate living at extremes, which is familiar and comfortable. All or nothing, good or bad, right or wrong, that's all there ever is for us.

Defenses are most often described by clients as "my wall" or "my armor." Both analogies lend themselves well to exploration in therapy. When it comes to our "walls", the dichotomy is either having to break them down or allowing them to stand. There's a lot that's lost in that perspective:

- The walls do not simply stand. It takes mental and emotional energy to maintain them
- The walls create distance between us and others, between ourselves and everything we most want.
- The wall blocks perspective and easily allows us to maintain constructs and false beliefs because the view never appreciably changes.
- How we treat ourselves behind the wall alternates between self-abuse and avoidance
- Our self-destruct button is on the inside of the wall – always within reach

In much the same fashion, "armor" is exhausting:

- Consider armor as a literal description. It's heavy, limits movement, and is cold.
- Armor is generally forged from pain
- Like walls, it only protects from external threats, when our biggest threat in adulthood is, more often than not, internal
- It's difficult to hug someone wearing armor

So, for those with walls, I scoff when they believe I'm asking to tear them down. There is no shortage of people we need to defend against in the world. To tear down the wall is to be largely defenseless. More importantly, we already know that the question of whether to tear them down is a rhetorical one.

The walls are supposed to provide a safe place where we can breathe and think. Instead, it's a place where we curl into the fetal position and obsess. The very idea that we can be safe alone for more than a brief period of solitude is inherently misguided. There is no more obvious truth than that people need people, yet here we are allowing our past experiences to convince us otherwise.

The very last thing we change is our expectations. Even when everything is different – even when the people in our lives today are nothing like those from our past, we secretly wait for them to reveal themselves to be Just. Like. Them.

Even when we're different, we expect the same mistakes, the same patterns to repeat and the same self-destruction to occur. It takes courage to have faith that things can be different, even when we have concrete proof that they are. This is one more reason why walls are limiting. Hiding behind them means the faith others have in us cannot permeate.

It is pure magical thinking to believe what we really want is for people to scale our walls. We're not Rapunzel in a tower. Build a fucking window so you can spot kindred spirits and then build a door to let them in.

Even the most fortified walls have cracks within them. Our clients can see through these cracks, but the images are shadowy and incomplete. Therapists know those cracks can be expanded, allowing greater light to shine in. We promote a sense of safety that facilitates curiosity. We offer reality checks about what's outside the wall and how it can be experienced and understood. We explore perspectives, determining and demonstrating how they're self-limiting. We help folks see and become more fully alive.

Doors are built slowly and with great patience. They too were once cracks. The healer will most often be the first safe person ever to enter. I'm fond of telling my clinicians that it is very often not what we do that makes a difference, but rather, who we are. I have too frequently been the first non-violent man, the first trusted confidant, the first that didn't want to simply take.

If I am safe, and my client is safe, then it becomes conceivable that others are, too. Doors are best built and opened by instinct. I urge my clients not to follow their hearts, for their hearts perceive things as we'd like them to be. The choice to open the door must always be made by our guts. We must have the courage to see people as they are, good or bad, and let them in or keep them out accordingly.

Boundaries are better than walls. They're flexible and protect without rigidity or self-limiting qualities. They're set according to need and they simplify absolutely everything. The key to setting them is the belief that we deserve their protection. It takes a lot of practice to get comfortable with this, and it first requires having a voice.

I urge every one of my clients to become progressively louder, more assertive, and more direct. Passive approaches don't work. Practice saying, "No." Practice saying, "Here is what I'm willing to do…and here is what I am not." Set limits. If we are consistent, good people adjust and bad people go away. We develop greater safety without running, hiding, or waiting to be rescued.

Many of us secretly hoped for fairy-tale endings to the pain that monsters inflicted and to the shame instilled within us. Our armor was subconsciously developed to defend us. More than that: it was designed to hold the fractionated self together. Broken but contained. Our fear of opening up is based in the fear of falling apart and, like Humpty Dumpty, never being put back together again.

How liberating would it be to trade our armor for a shield? Shields are lighter and only used as needed. Armor is forged from pain. By wearing it, we perpetuate our past and limit our present. Worst of all, there is always a gap in the armor – the opening the knife so easily slides into. It's no coincidence that the gap is always in the breast plate.

Shields, on the other hand, are consciously forged from light but durable metals: Identity, dignity, self-respect, and self-protection. A lot of unhealthy shit becomes difficult to do when you carry a shield. It's hard to let people walk on you unless you put it down. You can't be a sponge, and you can't take it on the chin anymore because that's the whole reason you built and carry it.

I don't have much use for armor or walls anymore. I am open to others like me. I can stand without them because even in the middle of the storm I remain true to myself. I carry a shield, and I allow my instincts and intuition to dictate with whom to use it. It took a lot of help to get here, and lots of support to stay here.

If I can, you can.

Never, Ever, See a Therapist on Friday Afternoons

I wear contact lenses. Sometimes they move around very slightly without my consent. It usually takes me a while to notice when this happens. I spend hours squinting and moving my eyes around, trying to bring the world back in focus. Sometimes I do that with my perspective too. Losing focus occurs when my priorities or self-care slip. Blaming it on stress or on being tired is bullshit. I'm not "stressed," I'm human. I'm not "tired," I'm trying to do too much.

I need to catch myself, or be caught by those closest to me, pretty quickly. If not, a low level, all too familiar depression comes on and seeps into every space in my world. Soon I feel myself just going through the motions, which for me is the worst feeling on earth. This is why I'd never see a healer on a Friday afternoon. I've been guilty more than a few times of "mailing it in" by then.

The quality I expected of myself used to conflict with the quantity I tried to provide. This was most evident in the number of clients I saw, a clear denial of my limitations. I'm eternally grateful to Mark Manson who put to words what I've learned over and over again through my career. In his book, The Subtle Art of Not Giving a Fuck, Manson explains the vitality of getting comfortable with ourselves and finding our true passions.

When you live as though you have a lot to prove, you care about a LOT of things and people. This is in no way manageable, and yet we try to manage it anyway. To live this way is to deny many obvious but unacceptable truths:

- The clients I saw on Wednesday got better stuff than the clients I saw on Friday
- My morning clients got better stuff than the right after lunch/I need a nap clients.
- The ongoing toll to my physical health (sleep deprivation, massive caffeine, and nicotine intake)
- The compassion fatigue that occurred by caring for everyone but me

Perversely, I took pride in the number of clients I could see in a week. For a long time, I saw almost twice the number of clients I'd ever allow an employee of mine to see today. As if that weren't more than enough, on nights and weekends I did on call community-based crisis intervention work. In retrospect, it's a laughable shit show of fear masquerading as pride.

Run, rabbit, run.

So of course, no matter where you go, there you are. While we all know that running away from ourselves is an exercise in futility, we alternate between running toward and coming back from burn out. Facing ourselves is, we believe, optional. But eventually, I was out of options. Being sick and tired of being sick and tired meant coming to terms with my demons and exorcising the fuckers.

Of course, they're not fully gone. They can come back any time I get one too many really great ideas. I occasionally ask my Higher Power what She's going to take away to offset all the cool stuff she adds. Then I experience the shitty epiphany that it's not a matter of what my HP is going to take away, it's about what I'm willing to let go of. I have been guilty over and over again of giving too many fucks. I've been forced to view this as I do my bank account: Don't write checks that can't be cashed. Balance is never achieved by robbing Peter to pay Paul.

I've eliminated tedious routines and dull duties. That has freed up a lot of time: I am happy to pay and exchange favors with others to do those things for me. This affords me more time to focus on what I love. I consciously allocated the time I got back into being a very active dad of young children, as well as a host of fulfilling pursuits and hobbies.

Having clarity about what I most care most about allows me to live by my priorities. I urge my clients and colleagues alike to define their own priorities for themselves. What are your priorities and where do you fall within them?

Answering the Tough Questions

Being a healer means folks will believe you're an expert on all manner of topics you know fuck-all about. It means folks will approach you as a moral authority, as a philosopher, as a spiritual guru, and as a behavioral scientist. Despite my best efforts to present myself as the freak I am, I am posed questions all day, every day, as to what's "normal." Why the fuck are you asking me? My bias is clear – normal is boring. Don't aspire to that. Considerations of morality are largely misguided as well. We can talk about what's good and bad—pointlessly, or we can talk about what works for you and what doesn't. I'd rather spend my time, and yours, doing the latter.

A lot of us get stuck in unanswerable and, worse, rhetorical questions. It's my goal to help people find their own answers, but whenever I'm asked tough questions, I'll often offer my truth as a starting point.

Amongst the slew of questions people have about God, the Universe, and everything is: "If there is a God, why would she/he/it have me be born to such terrible people." I have a theory about that. Like all my other theories it's remarkably simple:

Crazy people fuck and sometimes that makes a baby.

In my case, I'm pretty sure my parents were on a quest to redeem their horrible childhoods. I don't think a bearded man in the sky caused that. It happened, it sucked, and I dealt with it.

I grew up like most of us did - in a very unhealthy family that featured unpredictable outbursts of rage and denial of both needs and feelings. I learned the rules of an alcoholic family: don't speak, don't trust, don't be vulnerable. I grew up codependent. I didn't learn to care for others, I learned to *take care* of them. I learned that they could not be trusted to take care of themselves. Worse, I did not learn to take care of myself. I believed that to be a selfish thing as that's what my mother modeled for me. I identified with her subconsciously because I wanted to be the opposite of my father.

Adages ring true: It is not selfish to take care of yourself while serving the world. It is necessary. My problem was a product of not protecting what I wasn't taught to value. That's what a child learns when he's neglected at home and bullied in school. The takeaway is simple: "You don't matter."

The child is left with one of two choices: Prove them wrong or prove them right. Proving becomes a lifestyle. You do everything right, and it doesn't get you what you need. You do everything wrong, and no one stops you. Somewhere along the line, you choose a path. We chose honorably, but we whose lives are supposed to be proof of our worth don't practice self-care. We're too busy endlessly seeking to earn love and acceptance.

All of this creates a spiral. We don't burn out because of what we do. We burn out because of what we don't do. This reinforces the belief that we are not enough, which amplifies our shame, which leaves us trying harder and harder to do more and more. Nothing is sustainable because nothing is manageable.

I have learned that I can have far greater self-control through self-acceptance than I could ever have by being endlessly self-critical and rejecting of self. It's funny – we wear our hearts on our sleeves, carry the weight of the world on our shoulders and shoot ourselves in the foot and somehow, we think it's all so cleverly hidden that no one can see it. We help others despite how we were raised and how we are and even still, all we see in the mirror is a person who is not enough.

Good news! You're wrong. Look around at the peers you admire. Don't listen to your heart telling you how wonderful they are. Listen to your gut and recognize that they're fucked up, too, like we all are. The only distinction is that some of us are trying to get better and others are pretending we're fine, but in truth we're F.I.N.E. (Fucked up, Insecure, Neurotic and Evasive).

Stop making comparisons, and instead find kindred spirits who are seeking health. The take away from our comparisons only acts as a reinforcement of how much we suck. What's missed in this lose/lose scenario is that the comparison itself is not at all valid.

In short, we compare our insides to other people's outsides and make very problematic assumptions about how they feel and what they believe based on how they outwardly seem.

We overlook the obvious. They're pretending too. Trust me on this – if you could examine their insides you'd see something very different from the outside appearance. You'd be filled with empathy to discover that they hurt too, they feel insufficient, and they think far more highly of you than you do.

Writing:
- What're your means of self-control?
- How could you improve it?

F'ed Up and Fed Up

The closer I come to burnout, the more distance exists between me and those who love me. There's an adage in recovery, "If the distance between you and God has increased, ask yourself, who moved?"

"Lead us not into temptation but deliver us from evil." That's a remnant from my religious upbringing, and it's insane. I don't need a devil on my shoulder to tempt me. I fuck things up just fine all by myself. Worse, to deliver me from evil would most often mean to protect me from myself – from my own brokenness. I don't think my HP works that way.

She just waits with infinite patience for me to get off the latest self-appointed crusade and return to doing things Her way.

"...though I walk through the valley of the shadow of death, I will fear no evil for thou art with me."

God is always with me. The important but rhetorical question is, "Who is the bastard that keeps putting me in these valleys? I know my well-worn paths of self-destruction well, but I'm at least half way down them before I get honest with myself and others.

How readily we become lost simply by lying to ourselves about where we're headed.

I know it's a lot, but I'm on top of it. I'm fine. I'm fine. I'm fine. <minor glitch> I'm fucked.

I recognize my foibles anew each time I trip over them. I love my kryptonite. Cigarettes, caffeine, and achievements are my addictions.

In my mind, if I can, then I should. I'm drawn to people who are fucked up like me. I readily see their wounds and attend to them. I am drawn to pain, and I'm good at not taking it on as my own. I open doors for others who are broken like me, but I don't always pay attention to the supply of the good stuff coming into and out of me. That balance is a safeguard I cannot be without. Today I lose it only briefly and then refocus.

I taught others to expect everything of me, and I sought little or nothing in return. This was all part of my defensiveness and avoidance of self.

If I were of great service to you, you would love me. If you loved me, then you would not hurt me. Ideally, you'd tell others about me and in so doing, you'd spread the word that I am lovable.

I got a high from clients getting better, but like all highs it was fleeting, and like all addicts I was insatiable. Inevitably I became both drained and resentful. It's the cost of being too much to too many. I need a balance of reciprocity to avoid burnout.

The worst thing about burnout is the sense of déjà vu. That knowledge of having been in this hole before, and the realization that I alone put myself there. Same rut, same pattern, same bullshit that I mind fucked myself into believing: I'm not running from me. I'm not tripping over inconvenient truths. I'm not falling apart.

I only recognized the familiar pain when it refused to be ignored any longer.

My accountability got pushed aside when I was overextended. I easily justified it because I was busy <u>working</u>, doing <u>important</u> things. The world <u>needed</u> me, I didn't. I prioritized everyone else's recovery and then become increasingly resentful that my needs weren't being met.

Then came the self-pity. I am a world class martyr, always ready to throw myself under the bus then feel bad for myself for having tire marks on my forehead.

Eventually I became mindful that it did no good to get angry at myself. Beating myself up for being a mess just led me to dive into the next pitfall. It's crazy – I punished myself for being mean to myself, which is of course, mean. That's how easy it is to repeat the patterns in a losing battle for self-control.

Resolution isn't achieved by me fighting with me. I simplified by asking myself, "What would my HP have me do?"

Then I made realistic and sustainable commitments to myself, and I never waver from them. I invest in good food, good friends, hobbies outside of work, friendships and my marriage. Balance remains elusive. I am still a work in progress. I get sick of me sometimes. I hate finding the next layer of the goddamned onion to peel back. I'm just always glad when I get to the other side. It's worth it. I'm worth it.

I go back to basics. The surest way to not get lost is to let the Universe guide me and to tell folks where I'm at.

Questions you're likely to hate:
- What are your experiences with burnout?
- What are the commitments you've made to you?
- What prevents you from having greater self-care?
- How realistic are your expectations around vicarious and secondary trauma?

Good Crazy

I have a clear and bizarre memory of my parents explaining some research that emerged in my adolescence in which it was hypothesized that it takes three generations to breed depression out of a family tree. I thought that a life sentence at the time, but I think it's bullshit now. There are manageable and honorable ways to be nuts, and that's what I strive for.

The more I connect with folks on similar journeys, the more manageable mine becomes. My informal research has shown that one person out of every ten may be well worth knowing. Let's refer to these folks as "good crazy." With the notable exception of my wife, people I gravitate towards are various stages of broken and have highly addictive personalities.

My wife is what Shel Silverstein called my "Missing Piece." Our marriage is proof that not only do opposites attract, but they can also create inseparable bonds. She's a very healthy person who inexplicably adores me. She reels me in constantly, puts sweat and tears into making my dreams come true, and balances out my over the top nature with a grounded, steady presence.

I was at a high stakes poker game recently when an acquaintance took me to task for my position of discouraging people I like from drinking alcohol. He's young, so I patiently asked him to consider what percentage of poker players have addictive personalities? He came to the obvious answer: 100% of us.

Of the many things I do well, leaving a poker game is not one of them. The paradox about poker is that if you're any good at the game, you invest 6-12 hours at a time being bored with bursts of adrenaline interspersed. That's the high. That's the thing that makes you feel alive, and that's why poker is like life.

It's too often boring, and so you take some risks and balance them with investments to make it interesting. Maybe they pay off. Maybe they don't. Either way, you keep looking for the next high. Most people play poker the same way they live. I take a lot of risks professionally and personally, but I do so with standards for self-protection and self-care that I do not allow myself to deviate from because that would lead to madness in a hurry.

I maintain a slush fund for poker and never lose more than I can readily afford to. I maintain organizational habits and a level of healthy behaviors that I am completely committed to. I wish I had arrived at these from inspiration or some form of self-love. The truth is they were born from desperation. I burned out enough times to learn what it takes not to burn out.

Every day, come hell or high water, I will drink half a gallon of water, eat good food, and take time to rest. I maintain habits that ensure that I always know where things are, my schedule is always filled out, my cell phone is always charged and contains all the info I need for the day ahead. I walk every day. I do a ton of other little things that ensure the cheese stays on my cracker. I am not organized by nature, but rather, by necessity.

These are the most foundational aspects of maintaining a semi-healthy lifestyle that I consciously choose. If you're looking for an ideal to strive towards, it's not me. I'm a heavy smoker swilling Red Bull with an insatiable need to elevate my mood. I'm just lucky that I don't enjoy most drugs (other than caffeine, nicotine, and poker) and I get high off being of service to others.

You're like me. You may not be addicted like I am, or you may get off on different things, but you wouldn't be seeking to be more effective as a healer or helper if you weren't on some level, fucked up. I urge you to accept your fuckedupedness—rather than trying to hide or deny it—and make some conscious decisions going forward. How about:

- Heal what you can (shut up and go to therapy – get an objective opinion on you)

- Whatever things you can't or won't resolve, make conscious choices about how you're going to live with them. Take a long, hard, and honest look at your vices and consider what you would tell a client about them. (Write that shit down—do NOT do it in your head).
- Make some investments (tedious though they may be) to ensure a minimal level of self-care and self-protection. (Learn how to say no, how to set solid boundaries, and do at least a handful of things to be healthier physically and more organized in your daily life).

<u>Get what you need</u>

I just got back from a visit to my primary care physician. The good news is I'm only two weeks late in going to see him. There was a time when I would have pushed something like this off for months. I tolerate pain too well and if I can bear it, I probably will. I tell myself the same lies when I want to avoid something:

- It's not a big deal (because it's only my need, not someone else's)
- "I'm too busy to deal with it." (It = me)
- "It'll go away if I ignore it."

My healthier perspective today is a product of two negative experiences (being sick leads to being well).

In 1999, while going to college full time, working full time, being a homemaker/dad full time and never sleeping, I got seriously ill.

I crawled to the bathroom and spent five days on a couch sleeping almost 20 hours a day. It humbled me. For the first time in my life, I had limits. I was 31, and I'd never really learned to take care of myself. It changed me. I started eating better and sleeping more than 4 hours a night. These investments seemed monumental at the time. Today they are part of what I maintain as an absolute minimum standard for my self-care.

The second experience circled around events immediately prior and following becoming an amputee. I knew my leg was gone long before my doctors came to acceptance of it. I got the consults, saw the surgeon and scheduled what would turn out to be a 50-day hospital stay. The weekend before my surgery was pure hell. I can tell you with complete certainty that I know what a ten on the pain scale feels like. It's simple – I'd rather die than continue being in that much pain. That's what ten feels like. It's damned humbling to experience that. I can hurt so much that I'd rather not live? It's a level of discomfort that most of us never experience, but trust me—it exists. The drugs took the pain away until the doc took my leg away. The phantom pain that followed served as a multipurpose metaphor. It represented the pain of loss. The ache of what's missing. The parts of me that are broken and will never completely mend. Darkly amusing that phantom pain is one of the few places I've succeeded in doing therapy on myself.

The first time I felt it I knew what it was. I pulled back the hospital sheet and stared long and hard at where my lower leg used to be. I said aloud, "My right calf hurts. I no longer have a right calf; therefore, I refuse to accept pain from it." I repeated this process for two weeks, and the pain went away and has not recurred. I repeated the same process later on, when I felt a phantom itch on my nonexistent right foot, and it resolved.

So here's the thing about being a work in progress and getting better: Maybe you do a lot of the same crazy and self-limiting shit you've always done, but you do it for shorter and shorter periods of time and with less intensity. In my twenties I never went to a doctor, even when there was a very clear need. In my thirties, I went rarely and, in my forties, I go after about two weeks of discomfort.

It works the same way with my mental health. It's not like I never shame myself or beat myself up. I do it for a minute or two, and then I catch it. That's how mindfulness works – you pay attention to your shit, you notice yourself sliding into old thought patterns and behaviors, and you make conscious choices as to what the fuck you're going to do about that. I never in the full light of day said, "I'm going to ignore that." I told myself I'd come back to it or do it after I took care of far more important things (other people). I was lying. I had no intention of coming back. I kept hoping it would go away.

Decades later, I've learned that the only things that go away on their own are things you can't standing losing. A few good friends and some opportunities – those are the things I lost by neglect. Avoidance is a shitty thing to do to yourself. It creates room for dread, which is experiencing pain before pain actually arrives. It's a form of self-torture, and completely needless.

I love the recovery expression, "Pain is inevitable, and suffering is optional." I choose not to suffer. I find no joy in being a martyr as I once did. I have found that I cannot simultaneously caretake while being honest with myself.
All the dysfunctional shit we do is a form of settling for less than we can have. I have come to see that settling cannot be done honestly. You have to mind fuck yourself into believing it's all you deserve, all that's possible, or that trying for anything more would be too great a risk.

Fuck that. My brain goes old school, and I hear Freddy Mercury singing, "I Want It All." I'm willing to work for it. I'm willing to be patient with others and myself. I am not willing to be stagnant, complacent, or arrive at some final destination. I am more than a bit of a hedonist. I want everything this life has to offer, and I damned well deserve it.

Do you begrudge me that? No? Good. So why do you begrudge yourself? Don't let your brain turn that into a rhetorical question.

Grab pen and paper:
- Where are you settling?
- What do you do that's self-limiting?
- What would you do if you weren't afraid?
- What exactly do you deserve?

Unfucking Yourself

Recovery from burnout requires Rest, Relaxation, Release, and Reexamination. To rest and relax is foreign to many of us. We derive our sense of self-worth from the things we do, rather than who we are, so we only feel as good as what we've accomplished today. We must convince ourselves to view rest and relaxation as investments. We do better work when we're rested. We do better by the people in our lives when we're rested. We do better by ourselves when we're rested.

Why, then, are we so resistant to the very idea?

When we hit the wall, everything we have not released is right there with us. All the stress, anxiety, anger, and disappointments we repressed are all still a part of us. Everything we thought a nightcap took care of is still festering. Release is venting with the intention of letting go. It's journaling, having heart to hearts with dear friends and family, crying, laughing, and cursing. Give yourself an afternoon of voluntary Tourette's.

Reexamination is the most important piece. Left to our own devices, we'll come back from sick leave or that all too rare vacation and do the same crazy shit all over again. Sooner or later we are forced to consider exactly what we expect of ourselves. This is uncomfortable, because it forces us to see that we've been trying to do is either impossible, or takes too great a toll.

Intellectually we know we have limits, but emotionally we find limitations unacceptable. We believe that what it means to be a good worker/mother/daughter/friend/partner means that whatever the need is, we must meet it, regardless of what it costs us.

Conversely, we who do so much for so many expect too little in return. This creates an unsustainable inequity. Too much going out; too little coming in. What sustains us? What prevents us from doing something crazy like asking for help?

Funny thing about us – as long as we can stand it we will. When I couldn't do it anymore, I developed minimal standards that I never allow myself to deviate from. Come hell or high water, these are some things I make happen:

- Minimum of 7 hours of sleep a night
- Minimum of 4 vacations a year
- Daily spiritual practices
- Vitamins and supplements
- Time connecting with my wife
- Time spent every week with those who do what I do, talking about the work and what it costs us.

Choosing your minimal standard is a viable strategy for increasing stability, reducing stress, improving the quality of your life and breaking out of patterns that lead to burnout.

- Okay, so this sounds nice but will you actually make a minimal commitment to self?
- Grab pen and paper right now and make yourself some promises. My challenge to you is to stick the paper on your fridge and follow it daily.

Coffee with my conscience

I'd heard glowing things about a local therapist named Keith. His reputation alone made me want to know him. I waited in hopes that our paths would cross. That kept not happening, so on a slow day, I went looking for his profile online. I found tons of info about his practice and a lot of great reviews. There was one peculiarity, though – I couldn't find an email address for him. I was confounded. Who the hell keeps their email private these days?

So, I wrote to Keith the old-fashioned way. I sent a letter. Yeah, no shit, right? Within a few days he emailed me, and we made plans to meet for coffee.

Not five minutes into coffee, my soul screamed, "I want him to be my therapist!" For better and for worse, Keith suffered the same epiphany. We had connected, but upon confessing our desires, found ourselves at an impasse—there was no way for us to be *each other's* therapist. We both laughed and agreed that the only thing to do was to become friends.

It's been too rare for me to have someone like him in my life. In a world full of people that I find disappointing, Keith can challenge me. He's intelligent, empathic, sensitive, and aware. He's on my level. Maybe that sounds arrogant, but so be it. I'm at a point in my career and in my life where I've accepted that I can't talk about me without upsetting folks who feel less than.

I think of Marianne Williamson who eloquently describes how our playing small does not serve the world. One of the things I value most about my friends is that I can speak freely about my work and my experiences without concern for triggering their insecurities about their own work. That's the key – we need to relate to people who do what we do but we need for them to be healthy enough that our successes don't bother them, and our struggles don't threaten them.

Such healers are rare, and when I've met them, I most often hire them. This creates a dynamic in which I am less likely to be open about my current needs because these are folks I am far more focused on investing in than seeking from. What's delightful is that sometimes the student surpasses the teacher, and the relationship then becomes more egalitarian and reciprocal.

We need people to bounce ideas off of. We need collaboration and brainstorming. Without these things, we are left to our own devices and rely too heavily on old habits. Two heads aren't twice as good as one – they're exponentially better. Over years of collaborating, I developed the humility to support growth without insisting that my staff do exactly as I do. I have supervised clinicians whose styles are very different than mine, and I have learned from each of them.

Active peer supervision is something most don't aggressively seek. Having been educated and trained in competitive models, we only look to those who have more experience and expertise than we do. We would do well to take the advice we give to our clients. We urge them to seek natural supports and to avoid reinventing the wheel. When we seek together, we find more. When we struggle together, we feel far less alone.

The vulnerability inherent in peer support is the biggest barrier to collaboration. The person you hope to be promoted over is not the person you're likely to confide or break down with. This makes networking with outside professionals necessary. Ideally, it is only our organizations that are competing and not us individually. To offer or solicit peer supervision and support is far from foreign but it's certainly not mainstream. Agency culture is too often similar to our family of origin – we don't share what's happening with those outside the system.

Worse, agencies often actively discourage sharing by instilling an absolute paranoia about violating confidentiality. The truth is, it's not at all difficult to deidentify a client and seek consultation formally and informally. The HIPPA police will not come for you and your license. Seek out folks who know more than you do. Seek out folks who have congruent needs and struggles.

We don't need to get together to complain about the organizations we work for. That's generally a lose/lose proposition that devolves quickly into frustration over powerlessness. Let's move our focus to sharing our needs and our knowledge. Not only is this more productive, but it feels a hell of a lot better than kvetching.

It's humanizing, and a safeguard against burnout, to share exactly where we're at. We're able to offer each other suggestions and reality checks. We're able to bear witness to one another's struggles and victories alike. We need to move beyond the idea that we don't have time for these types of undertakings and toward the idea that these investments enhance the quality of our work and our lives.

Let Go or be Dragged

I've encountered relatively few authors I can enjoy on topics of spirituality. Anne Lamott, Richard Rohr, and Elizabeth Gilbert are amongst the few who don't sound like fake people to me. I need to hear from people who are really real and who say things like, "Here's how I dealt with being mad as hell with God" or "Here's how I came to choose some truth that works for a fucked-up person like myself."

Spirituality is connection. Connection is everything. It's belonging and relating. It's being valued, understood, empathized with, believed in, and meaningfully supported. To receive all the benefits of connection, though, I have to be constantly willing to connect to myself.

We know to take holistic and person-centered approaches with those we serve, but not with ourselves. Being connected to self means being aware of and invested in our physiological, mental, emotional, and spiritual well-being. For me, that means a combination of mindfulness and healthy habits – commitments that I maintain no matter what is going on around me.

Even still, sometimes I run from myself. Sometimes I hide. I've gotten worlds better at avoiding avoidance, but I don't want to be the only one who is monitoring what's really going on within me. Even when things are good, that's just too much work. Further, I've accepted that beyond brief and fleeting times of solitude, the only thing I can be without connection is profoundly alone in a world that feels very, very cold.

I've come to accept that if I am to continue bearing witness to pain, then I have two choices: I can burn out, or I can continue to grow spiritually.

What Were You Saying About God?

With regard to God, the Universe, and everything...I like simplicity there too. In addition to all the other ways in which I'm screwed up, I also happen to be a minister's son. I was raised in several different denominations of Christianity, none of which worked for me at all.

I have a great affinity for <u>dis</u>organized religion. When misfits share their experience, strength, and hope that's what spirituality is to me. It's connections to good people, ideas, and shared experiences. Through our ability to empathize, we relate, identify, and we say the two most spiritual words people can say: Me too.

I do not believe I am so clever as to have located and engaged the misfits in my life. I choose to believe that something far more powerful than me facilitates that. I refer to my HP as the Universe because it feels more inclusive, and carries fewer connotations, than saying, "God."

I have served countless folks who sought God in books. I've only ever known one person who believed they succeeded at this. Shortly after meeting me, my intellectualized new friend told me he'd been studying comparative religion for over thirty years.

Without thinking, I asked him, "What do you do with all that knowledge?"

He stared at me for a long moment before admitting, "It never occurred to me that I'd *do* something with it."

I'm humble enough to admit I have an extremely limited understanding of "God," and moreover to be comfortable with that fact. I can't understand how the engine in my car runs. What hope do I have of understanding my HP? So I don't seek to understand. I seek to experience. I've seen too many miracles not to have faith that there is something. My belief system is second only to the Dali Lama in simplicity. He said, "My religion is simple. My religion is kindness." I say I believe there is something. I choose to believe that it cares about me. I talk to It the way I'd talk to a friend, and it keeps working out really well. I do not believe that talking to my HP changes in any way what my HP does or is. Rather, it makes me more aware of and receptive to the good things that appear in my path.

I believe there is a strong connection between what I know intuitively and what I know spiritually. I laugh at my clients who say they'd like a burning bush to guide them, as if they'd believe that it was the Universe talking to them and not simply a psychotic episode. The God of my understanding works through other people. The more misfits I'm connected to, the easier it is to hear what I need to hear and envision the course of action I am to take.

As a young man, I read the Celestine Prophecy. It was a terrible book with two great ideas: First, there are no coincidences (everything is potentially meaningful). Second, in every meeting, ask yourself, What do I have to offer you and what do you have to offer me? We'd do well to approach each other with awareness of what we have to offer and what we need to receive. We're here to teach and love each other. In the end, relationships and experiences are all that matter anyway.

Most of us remain agnostic as a means of avoidance. I devote more energy to trying to get folks to believe in themselves and to find their tribe than I do to trying to convince them to have faith in a Higher Power. My experience is that doing those two things naturally results in a person growing spiritually.

Shame is the greatest obstacle to spiritual growth. I've had plenty of folks say some variation of, "There may very well be a God, but what would he want to do with someone as horrible as me?" I point out that nearly every major religion has a story of redemption that explains how humans became deserving of our creator's attention and love. If the need for redemption is that universal, then it really wouldn't matter if some of us are better than others, because none of us are deserving.

I want to open doors for my clients, and so I attack shame. Typically, every reason we're ashamed is one of three things: a lie, a product of what was done to us, or something we regret. People in recovery do not judge one another for their pasts. Our pasts do not define us. Who we're working to be today does.

If we can remove shame, then we can allow others to serve us. We can develop healthy friendships and supports. The sheer volume of possibilities this creates is spiritual in and of itself. Ultimately, we become open to new ways of living and choose progressively healthier paths.

Healing and recovery processes allow us to hear what works for others. Many will give credit to their HP. Sooner or later, we come back around sooner or later to whether or not there's a God. Deep down we're afraid to choose because we're afraid that if we get it wrong, we go to hell. As my friends in AA say, "Religion is for people who are afraid to go to hell and spirituality is for those of us who have already been there."

I don't believe in hell as an afterlife. I could never reason that the all-loving, all-forgiving and all-knowing God of religion could send people to an eternity of suffering. Realistically, I don't see myself living past 80. Let's say for the sake of argument that I fucked everything up throughout my life. A trillion years of suffering would only be a drop in the bucket of my eternal damnation.

Like a loving God wouldn't come get me after 80 years and offer another shot at getting it right? AA's literature offered me the concept of a "God of my understanding." I reason that if God is truly infinite, then all explanations of God are accurate. Pick what works for you and have the guts to follow it.

I think William Blake was on to something when he said, "Faith is a bet you can't lose." If I believe in something that brings me more peace, purpose, love, or joy, even if I'm wrong, so what? I'll end up just as dead as I would be otherwise.

How about you?
- Do you know what you believe?
- How does it guide you and make your life more meaningful?
- How could it further support your growth?

The Golden Rule in Reverse

Most healers and helpers are not nearly as self-accepting as we are accepting of others. We celebrate diversity while believing we're freaks. We do not care for ourselves nearly as well as we do for others. We uphold the value of oppressed people and too often devalue ourselves and our efforts.

In the midst of all we seek to change, may we achieve greater awareness of our own needs and have a greater willingness to meet them. May we notice the ways in which we oppress ourselves and seek both lovingly and pragmatically to overcome them.

Here is the great overlap between healing and social justice: Ideas alone do very little. They don't improve people's lives. It's the application of ideas that makes the difference. Expanding awareness and educating are always beneficial, but if we don't get down to the concrete aspects of how to evoke change, then all we've done is make people more aware of their suffering and limitations.

Most of what we need to change is done subconsciously. No one ever consciously reasons, "I think I'll spend the next 15 minutes revisiting every significant failure and tell myself that my past defines me." No one believes it's productive or useful to call themselves an idiot. Beating ourselves up is reactive and reflexive—we do it without thought. What we do for others runs the gamut between codependent and effective as hell. What we do reflexively to ourselves is neglect at best and varying levels of self-abuse at worst.

Simple Lessons:
- Mindfulness is just a nice word for, "Pay attention to you."
- Practice the Golden Rule in reverse
- Take the advice you give
- Whenever you're unsure, what would you tell a patient?

Shut up and do the work

As a therapist, the most liberating advice I've received came from Mary Pipher, author of "Reviving Ophelia," the book that revolutionized the treatment of adolescent girls and young women. For all her brilliance, Pipher is humble. In her book "Letters to a Young Therapist," she refers to herself as a "meat and potatoes therapist." Her point in saying this is that encouraging people to take care of the basics is always our strongest move.

The basics: nutrition, good sleep, hydration, exercise, time with people who matter.

The more skeptical part of my brain references Kurt Vonnegut, who said that the problem with the world is that "everybody wants to build, and nobody wants to do the maintenance work." So, I'll meet you half way. If you're not going to hit the gym, then just say so. Stop whining about it. Stop shaming yourself for what you should be doing and put your energy into what you're willing to do.

If ever you see me at a gym it will be a sure sign that something has seriously gone awry. I hate everything about gyms, and I'm just fine with that. In my pursuit of maintaining a series of commitment to myself, instead of going to the gym I walk every day. I resolved this by noting that my anguish over the gym had been going on for years without me ever actually going to the gym. What I've gleaned from that experience is that agony is always optional. I don't ever have to do it, but the alternative is to develop conviction over what I am willing to do.

So, I walk. I don't walk because I especially enjoy it. I walk because I don't want to keep buying bigger pants. I'm ambivalent about walking, but I really hate buying clothes. That's how hard it is to tilt the scales and make a choice. Even if I'm picking the lesser of evils, it's still a choice. The point is to focus on what you are willing to do, do it, and get on with your life.

In short, the point is: Do what you will, but do it on fucking purpose. If you're willing to eat salad for lunch then do that, and if you're still going to eat chips and chocolate after 10 pm then fuck it, that's what you're going to do. The salad still helps, and you can always add a daily multivitamin.

The potential add-ons to your self-care are endless, and yet you're more likely to focus on stuff you don't want to do. Add something fun: massage therapy, hot tubs, saunas. Stop thinking of these as indulgences or lavish expenses. Make an investment that pays off in talk therapy, art classes, Reiki, Qi-gong, martial arts. Make plans for things to look forward to: Buy non-refundable plane tickets to ensure you'll take the damned vacation.

The Vitality of Fun

We know that "all work and no play makes Jack a dull boy." What we overlook is that it also burns him the fuck out. We treat fun like it's optional, or even frivolous, and this makes compassion fatigue all the more likely. Laughter is release. It's cathartic. It helps us to make "lighten up" a feasible proposition instead of an empty ideal. It helps us to take ourselves less seriously and to know that there is joy in the midst of the darkness.

We're half-assed in our pursuit of fun. We tend to only be active in our use of gallows humor to cope. Fun is something <u>we have to go out and do</u>. That leaves us two options: close connections to folks who are spontaneous, or planning. Having something to look forward to makes stressful times more manageable

The best people I've known can have a good time at the DMV. If you allow yourself just to be yourself, a million things become possible. When we're in the moment and authentic, we laugh more, dance more, take more risks and live more fully. Double your misery back if not satisfied.

Laugh with your clients. Find the levity. Teach folks how to laugh at themselves in a way that isn't self-deprecating. Every form of mental illness and self-destruction robs us of fun. Help them to find what's fun for them. If you're not sure how to do this, watch Robin Williams perform. Don't focus on how it ended for him. Learn from what kept a man with severe mental illness, cocaine addiction and alcoholism alive for over six decades.

Humor is coping in the workplace

One of the wisest individuals I have ever known was a coworker who referred to herself as, "just a poor little old black lady who don't know nothing and don't have no fancy degrees." This lady had a remarkable gift for finding the humor in any given situation. In the rare times when there wasn't anything to laugh about, she'd make it up, because she knew: Laughter is proof that it's going to be okay.

We worked together every Friday afternoon. Anyone who has ever worked in crisis services knows that Friday 5 pm is the witching hour. It's the time when people who have resources and the authority to make decisions go home, and those of us who put band-aids on gaping wounds take over. My friend and I encountered an insufferable amount of incompetency working in the public sector. She would deal with this by discovering a person's quirks and developing innovative strategies to fuck with them.

This became a game for us. The challenge was for me not to laugh and one up her by saying something even more preposterous. The greatest of all such encounters was a discussion of our colleague's weekend plans that centered around, "Mr. Johnson." Now, Mr. Johnson was a Labrador retriever, and I'm sure a very fine one at that. Our colleague was blissfully unaware that "Johnson" is a slang term for penis.

My friend (who is evil in the very best of ways) asked how she and Mr. Johnson would spend the evening together? Our coworker explained that they would be going to Burger King because all the girls at Burger King love Johnson and they know exactly how he likes his meat prepared. My friend reacted to this as though it was the most scandalous and seductive thing she'd ever heard and demanded an in-depth description. She gyrated and breathed, "Mmm, hmmm" after each detail. I managed to keep a straight face and feign great interest throughout the encounter. We lost our shit for a full ten minutes after our colleague left. It was silly and perhaps childish, but it was a viable means to cope, and we weren't hurting anyone. Laughing so hard that you cry and your sides ache is the best form of spirituality.

Letting Go

I just finished having lunch with someone I greatly admire. She is one of a handful of especially wonderful people that can truly challenge me. I told her about a meeting I had recently with a colleague I support. My message to him was that he needed to let go of being overly responsible and increase his self-care. She shot me a wicked grin and asked what it was that I needed to let go of.

She's looking at my blind side and seeing the things that I can't and won't consider. She suggested that I need to let go of the fears I have around this book and other projects I hold dear. Sage advice. Let it go and see what it will become. I have learned countless lessons about what happens when I try to control things, and still, I persist. My spirit and my mind say that if even a handful of folks benefit from my writing, then I have succeeded. My emotional self wants far more. It wants to be heard by huge numbers of people. If I apply rational/emotive therapy to myself, I can reasonably consider how many would be enough.

Except feeling "enough" is something I have struggled with throughout my life. I know and believe that I am. It is only the feeling of this that ebbs and flows. I am the first to attest that others are enough, and I am also quick to point out that it's okay to want more and become more.

So how do I manage to keep getting in my way?

Well, it's easy to do. I am presenting what is in effect not only my life's work, but also simply my life. I am weighing whether my example is likely to prove helpful to others. I am agonizing over whether it's well written. I've worked with three different editors, two of whom would make excellent therapists, and one of whom is an excellent therapist.

They've given me options instead of doing the work for me. They've encouraged me to bare my soul and maintain responsibility for every choice about how my stories are told. They've laughed with me about my hang-ups. So, this is one more time I practice what I preach.

I dare to dream greatly. I share my experience, strength, and hope openly. I hope you save yourself some strife by virtue of my mistakes.

Moreover, I hope you take excellent care of yourself and become not only increasingly effective in your work, but also more joyous in your heart. Blessed be.

Made in the USA
Columbia, SC
29 February 2020